THE FLORIDA
COOKBOOK

THE FLORIDA COOKBOOK
A Lighter Look At Southern Cooking

By Charlotte Balcomb Lane
Edited by Heather J. McPherson

A publication of The Orlando Sentinel
Sentinel Books
Orlando/1990

Written by Charlotte Balcomb Lane
Edited by Heather J. McPherson
Designed by Melissa Slimick
Cover photos by Tom Burton
Illustrations by Gerald Masters and Brenda Weaver
Production by David W. Wersinger
Printed in the United States by R.R. Donnelley
ISBN 0-941263-13-4

Lane, Charlotte Balcomb, 1956-
    The Florida cookbook : a lighter look at Southern cooking / by
Charlotte Balcomb Lane ; edited by Heather J. McPherson. — 1st ed.
        p.   cm.
    "A publication of the Orlando sentinel."
    ISBN 0-941263-13-4 : $18.95
    1. Cookery, American—Southern style. 2. Cookery—Florida.
I. McPherson, Heather J. II. Title.
TX715.2.S68L36   1990
641.59759--dc20

About the author

Award-winning food writer and columnist, Charlotte Balcomb Lane began cooking for fun while still a teen-ager in Albuquerque, N.M. She got her first taste of professional cooking as a sandwich maker in a pub in Leuven, Belgium, where she was a foreign exchange student for a year after high school.

After returning to the United States, Lane spent several years working as a baker and caterer. She eventually opened her own international foods catering service.

Lane graduated from the University of New Mexico in 1982 with a degree in journalism. She wrote restaurant reviews and feature stories for the Food section of the *Albuquerque Journal* before taking a position as a catering manager at a Four Seasons hotel in Dallas. Lane joined the staff of *The Orlando Sentinel* in 1986, and writes two columns for the newspaper's Food section. "Eating for Life" offers readers heart-healthy recipe ideas and "The Global Gourmet" focuses on ethnic cooking. She is married to Peter Lane, a native Floridian and wine consultant.

This book goes out to all the kind hearts and willing hands who have helped make it a reality, especially my loving husband, Peter, who encourages me in all my cooking adventures.

Acknowledgements

This book would not have been possible without the help of many talented people. The author and the editor are grateful for the support and guidance of the following:

Special thanks goes to Betty Boza and Phyllis Gray of the Orlando Sentinel test kitchen staff. Their copious notes and suggestions on the recipe procedures were invaluable.

Robin Niedz, chief clinical dietitian at Winter Park Memorial Hospital, and Fabiola Gaines and Karen Brushwood, of her staff, analyzed all the recipes for nutritional content.

The creative team of Melissa Slimick, Gerald Masters, Brenda Weaver and David W. Wersinger brought this work to life through their designs and illustrations.

Tom Burton's beautiful cover photo captured the essence of this book. His patience during the world's longest photo shoot is deeply appreciated.

Dixie Kasper and April Medina's suggestions and encouraging words during the writing, editing and proofing stages kept us all on track.

And last, but not least, we sincerely thank Dana Eagles, George Biggers and Bethany Mott, who encouraged us to take on this project.

TABLE OF CONTENTS

Introduction

The Florida of the '90s is a far cry from the Florida Pulitzer-prize winning author Marjorie Kinnan Rawlings discovered in the '20s and eventually celebrated through her books *Cross Creek, The Yearling* and *Cross Creek Cookery.*

But the same spirit of adventure and the longing for new opportunities that drew Rawlings to Cross Creek still lures people to Florida from points near and far.

The result is that Florida has become a rich culinary melting pot of old ideas blended with new. Southern staples such as sweet corn, grits and seafood are being prepared in a myriad of ways.

The state's growing Puerto Rican, Vietnamese and Jamaican populations are expanding the Southern larder to include exotic spices and produce. And the native cooking techniques of these new residents are being integrated into Southern cooking as well.

The business boom in Florida has brought new residents from all over the United States, too. These newcomers have introduced other regional cuisines and incorporated Florida's seemingly endless harvest of produce into their menus.

The national trend toward more low-fat cooking is also having an affect on how Floridians eat. They may still insist on grits but not always doused in butter and salt. Jalapeno peppers, garlic and spice blends are gaining popularity as seasonings for these healthful grains. In fact, grits are just as likely to show up at brunch in the form of a low-calorie souffle as they are as a breakfast side dish.

Barbecue is still king, but the backyard get-togethers are likely to include grilled chicken or seafood served with skewered vegetables as heart-healthy options to a meaty slab of ribs. And while cole slaw is still being passed at the table, it may not be bound with calorie-laden mayonnaise and salad dressings.

When Rawlings bought her Alachua County cottage in 1928, Florida cuisine was synonymous with Cracker cooking, a reference to the cracking sound made by the whips of pioneering cattle ranchers. Their menus generally included cornmeal batters, fried fish and chicken, barbecued beef and fresh greens.

Considering all the changes that have taken place, is it time for a new definition of Florida food?

In true pioneering spirit, it probably is best not to restrain culinary creativity to words. Just as Florida has welcomed its new residents, kitchens from Miami to the Panhandle will always have room for a new spin on a Cracker favorite.

Heather McPherson

APPETIZERS

■ Flaky thin pastry and a delectable, cheese filling make this an extraordinary first course for a dinner party or a spring brunch.

Asparagus Strudel

12 sheets phyllo dough
(approximately 12-by-17 inches)

Non-stick cooking spray
(preferably olive oil)

16 spears of fresh asparagus

1 cup 1-percent low-fat cottage cheese

4 ounces feta cheese, crumbled

1 tablespoon grated Parmesan cheese

2 egg whites

2 tablespoons fresh dill, chopped or ¼ teaspoon dried dill

6 tablespoons fine, dry bread crumbs, divided (about ½ cup)

¼ teaspoon white pepper

¼ teaspoon salt

1 clove garlic, crushed

If phyllo is frozen, thaw in refrigerator overnight. Preheat oven to 325 F. Trim asparagus by bending each stem until it snaps. They should be about 4 inches. Reserve and finely chop remaining tender parts of stems. Discard woody parts. Cook tips in microwave oven on high (100 percent) power for 2 minutes; cool. Cook chopped stems in microwave oven on high for 2 minutes. Drain and cool.

In a bowl or a food processor, combine the cottage cheese, feta cheese, Parmesan cheese, egg whites, dill, 3 tablespoons of the crumbs, pepper, salt and garlic. Mix well. Add the chopped asparagus and mix again.

Assemble the phyllo, cooking spray, 3 tablespoons of crumbs, cheese filling and asparagus tips. Lay down two sheets of the phyllo in separate piles and spray each with cooking spray. Add another sheet of phyllo to each pile and spray with cooking spray. Sprinkle lightly with about ⅓ of the crumbs. Top with two more sheets of phyllo, spray lightly with cooking spray and sprinkle with crumbs. Continue until all phyllo and crumbs are used. Cut the stacks of sheets into quarters. Divide the cheese mixture over each quarter section of phyllo, leaving a 1-inch border. Place 4 spears of asparagus on cheese. Loosely roll each piece of phyllo; pinch ends to seal. Spray surface lightly with cooking spray. Place on a baking sheet. Bake for 30 minutes, or until dough is lightly brown. Serve each with Marinara Sauce (recipe 122) on the side.

Makes 8 servings.

Nutrition information per serving: calories, 199; fat, 3.7 grams; carbohydrate, 30 grams; cholesterol, 14.5 milligrams; sodium, 543 milligrams.

■ This Mediterranean-inspired appetizer spread is also great for a picnic at the beach. Serve with French bread and fresh fruit.

Tapenade Spread

1 (6¾-ounce) can water-packed tuna, drained
1 (2-ounce) can flat anchovies, drained and blotted free of oil
1 cup pitted black olives
¼ cup capers, drained
2 tablespoons olive oil
2 tablespoons cholesterol-free mayonnaise
1 tablespoon brandy
¼ teaspoon hot pepper sauce
Lemon and parsley for garnish (optional)

In container of food processor or electric blender combine tuna, anchovies, olives and capers; process with a pulsing motion for 3 or 4 seconds until mixture is blended, but not smooth. Put mixture in a mixing bowl; stir in oil, mayonnaise, brandy and hot pepper sauce. Spoon into serving bowl. Garnish with lemon slice and parsley, if desired. Serve with crackers or crudites.

Makes about 1 cup.

Nutrition information per tablespoon: calories, 59; fat, 4.1 grams; carbohydrate, 0.9 grams; cholesterol, 5 milligrams; sodium, 424 milligrams.

Fast facts

Your first step toward better nutrition begins in the grocery store. Shop for products that are low in fat, cholesterol, salt and sugar. In most cases, the savings in fat and calories are appreciable.

For example, a tablespoon of mayonnaise has 100 calories; a tablespoon of low-fat mayonnaise has only 45 calories.

■ Spicy-food lovers can add more fire to the dip with hot sauce or finely minced, fresh hot chilies. Save calories by dipping celery sticks instead of chips.

Chili con Queso

2 tablespoons olive oil
1 medium onion, chopped (about
    ½ cup)
1 (15-ounce) can tomatoes, well
    drained
1 (4-ounce) can chopped chilies,
    drained
⅓ cup skim milk
½ teaspoon hot pepper sauce
2 cups shredded Cheddar cheese
Unsalted tortilla chips

In medium saucepan heat olive oil and saute onion until tender. Add tomatoes, breaking up with a fork. Stir in chilies. Cover; simmer 15 minutes. Stir in milk and hot pepper sauce. Simmer 2 minutes longer; add cheese. Cook, stirring constantly, until cheese is melted and mixture is smooth. Serve immediately with tortilla chips.

Makes about 3 cups or 24 servings.

Test kitchen notes: To make this in the microwave oven, in a 2 quart microwave-safe bowl, heat oil and onion for 45 seconds on high (100 percent) power. Add tomatoes and chilies and cook for 3 more minutes on high. Stir in milk, hot pepper sauce and cheese. Cook for 1 minute on high, stir, and cook 1 more minute if needed to melt cheese. Cheese mixture should be smooth.

Nutrition information per serving without chips: calories, 56; fat, 4.3 grams; carbohydrate, 1.7 grams; cholesterol, 10 milligrams; sodium, 90 milligrams.

■ The sweetness of the roasted peppers and the brininess of the green olives make this a favorite party dip. It is light enough to serve year-round.

Red-Hot Dip

3 slices whole wheat bread
¼ cup skim milk
2 medium-size red bell peppers
¼ cup pitted green olives
1 clove garlic
2 tablespoons olive oil
1 tablespoon lemon juice
½ teaspoon hot pepper sauce
Sliced olives for garnish, optional

Break bread into a small bowl; add milk. Soak bread pieces for 10 minutes. Peel peppers by holding them over the heated burners of a stove until they are charred, or roast peppers over an outdoor barbecue grill until the skins are charred. Cool and peel peppers. In the bowl of a food processor or blender combine bread, peppers, olives and garlic. Process with a pulsing motion about 4 seconds, or just until combined. Add oil, lemon juice and hot pepper sauce; process

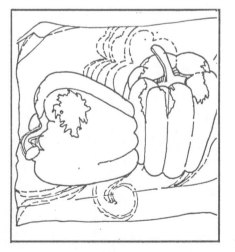

Step 1: Steam grilled or broiled peppers in a heavy plastic bag or covered bowl for 5 to 10 minutes.

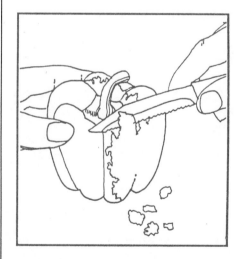

Step 2: Working from the stem down, remove charred skin with a paring knife.

about 3 seconds longer. Spoon into serving bowl. Cover. Let stand at least 30 minutes to blend flavors. Garnish with sliced olives, if desired.

Serve with pita bread, Herbed Pizza Dough (page 170) or fresh vegetables.

Makes about 1¼ cups or 12 servings.

Nutrition information per serving: calories, 42; fat, 2.7 grams; carbohydrate, 4.1 grams; cholesterol, 0 milligrams; sodium, 58 milligrams.

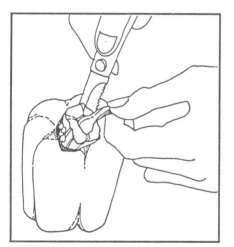

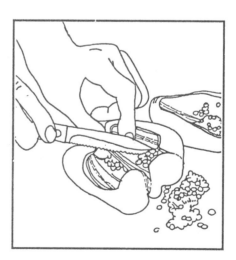

Step 3: Cut around stem with a paring knife and pull out the stem with core.

Step 4: Cut peppers in half and scrape away seeds and white pith (ribs).

■ Pack this versatile spread for outings at the lake or by the pool. It is a healthy snack that doesn't require refrigeration.

Greek Hummus Dip

1 (16-ounce) can garbanzos
   (chick peas), drained
½ cup non-fat plain yogurt
2 tablespoons tahini paste
1 tablespoon lemon juice
1 to 2 small cloves garlic, minced
¼ teaspoon ground cumin
2 teaspoons minced fresh or
   dried parsley
Pita bread, cut into triangles
Cucumber slices
Zucchini slices

Combine garbanzos, yogurt, tahini paste, lemon juice, garlic and cumin in food processor bowl of blender; process at high speed until smooth, stopping to scrape bowl occasionally. Stir in parsley. Spoon into serving bowl. Serve with pita bread and vegetables for dipping.

Makes 2 cups.

Test kitchen notes: Tahini paste, which is made from crushed sesame seeds, can be found in gourmet or ethnic food departments of many supermarkets or in Oriental grocery stores. Tahini should be stored in the refrigerator. If it is not available, tahini paste can be omitted. This recipe can be made up to 3 days in advance and stored in the refrigerator.

Nutrition information per serving (values will vary depending on how much dip adheres to food): calories, 31; fat, 0.8 grams; carbohydrate, 4.4 grams; cholesterol, 0 milligrams; sodium, 4.8 milligrams.

Fast facts

Dried beans and peas, such as chick peas, black beans, black-eyed peas and lentils, are excellent sources of soluble fiber. Soluble fiber, which is also found in oat bran, can lower your blood cholesterol, according to some studies. Made up of pectins and gums, soluble fiber traps cholesterol-forming biles so they can be excreted.

■ This delicious dip is flavorful but low in unhealthy fats. Serve it for every gathering of friends.

Black Bean Salsa

1 (16-ounce) can black beans, drained
1 (12-ounce) jar hot Mexican-style salsa
¼ cup fresh cilantro, chopped
¼ teaspoon cumin
2 tablespoons freshly squeezed lime or lemon juice
Unsalted tortilla chips
Jicama slices
Yellow squash slices

In a food processor or blender, roughly chop the black beans, being careful not to puree them into mush. Stir in the salsa, cilantro, lime juice and cumin. Refrigerate overnight to allow the flavors to blend. Serve with tortilla chips and sliced vegetables.

Makes 3 cups.

Test kitchen notes: This recipe was inspired by a Venezuelan recipe called caviar criollo or "native caviar."

Nutrition information per serving (values will vary depending on how much salsa adheres to food): calories, 15 ; fat, 0 grams; carbohydrate, 2.7 grams; cholesterol, 0 milligrams; sodium, 26.5 milligrams.

Even people who think they don't like tofu will enjoy it in this cheesy dip. People who already love low-fat tofu will adore it this way.

Blue Cheese Dip

1 clove garlic, peeled
8 ounces tofu, drained
3 tablespoons white-wine vinegar
½ cup non-fat yogurt
1 tablespoon skim milk
1 teaspoon Worcestershire sauce
4 ounces blue cheese, crumbled
Dash hot pepper sauce
Snow peas
Red pepper spears
Steamed sweet potatoes, chilled

Place the garlic in a blender or food processor. Process until garlic is finely chopped and add tofu, vinegar, yogurt, milk and Worcestershire sauce. Process until smooth. Add blue cheese and process briefly until cheese is lumpy. Add hot sauce to taste. Spoon into a serving bowl. Refrigerate until ready to serve.

Accompany with snow peas, peppers and steamed sweet potatoes.

Makes 2 cups.

Nutrition information per serving (values will vary depending on how much dip adheres to food): calories, 20.5; fat, 1.3 grams; carbohydrates, 0.5 grams; cholesterol, 2.7 milligrams; sodium,

■ Once you have tried unfried spring rolls, you may lose your taste for the heavier, fried versions. The flavor of vegetables, herbs and shrimp is delightful plain or with garlicky Nuoc Leo dipping sauce.

Vietnamese-Style Spring Rolls

2 ounces thin rice vermicelli
8 shrimp, peeled and deveined
8 ounces ground turkey
1 clove garlic, crushed through a
    press
1 tablespoon fish sauce
8 leaves red or green leaf lettuce
1 cup fresh bean sprouts
½ cup mint leaves
½ cup fresh cilantro
8 sheets rice paper (medium
    size)
Nuoc Cham (page 154) or Nuoc
    Leo (recipe follows)

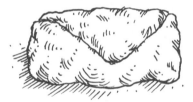

Bring 1 quart of salted water to a boil. Add the rice vermicelli and cook for 3 to 4 minutes; drain and set aside.

Cook shrimp in a microwave oven for 2 minutes on high (100 percent) power. Allow to cool. Slice in half lengthwise; set aside. Mix the ground turkey with the crushed garlic and the fish sauce. Crumble the mixture in the bottom of a microwave-safe baking dish. Cook on high power for 2 minutes. Stir and cook on high for 2 minutes longer, or until meat is no longer pink. (The meat also can be cooked in a non-stick skillet.) Set cooked meat aside and allow to cool.

Put rice vermicelli noodles on a cutting board and chop into 2-inch pieces. Combine the rice vermicelli and cooked ground turkey.

Arrange turkey and vermicelli mixture, lettuce, bean sprouts, mint leaves, cilantro and rice paper around a work space. Have a large shallow pan of hot water ready to moisten rice papers. Dip a sheet of rice paper into water. Allow it to soak for 30 seconds. Place it on the counter and allow it to stand until the paper becomes pliable.

Place 2 halved shrimp lengthwise across the middle of the rice paper. Lay a lettuce leaf, spine-side up, over shrimp like a blanket. Make sure the leaf is smaller than the rice paper.

Spoon about 2 tablespoons of the turkey mixture in a log shape on lettuce.

Lay about 2 tablespoons of the bean sprouts over the turkey. Top with several mint and cilantro leaves.

Fold the right side of the rice paper almost to the center. Fold the left side of the rice paper toward the center. Fold the bottom half toward the middle and roll into a tight cylinder. Continue to make rolls until all 8 are made. Serve with Nuoc Leo (recipe follows).

Rolls can be made 2 hours ahead. Cover with a damp towel and keep refrigerated until ready to serve.

Makes 4 servings.

Step 1: Put shrimp, lettuce and stuffing near center of rice paper (above).

Step 2: Fold the bottom of the rice paper to cover the stuffing.

Step 3: Fold the left and right sides of the rice paper toward the center. They should overlap just a bit.

Step 4: Continue to roll the bottom toward unfolded end.

Step 5: Rolled spring rolls are ready to arrange on serving plates.

Test kitchen notes: These delicate hors d'oeuvres are like egg rolls, but they are not fried. They are very fresh and light, especially dipped in the zesty Nuoc Leo. It may take practice to learn to roll them well.

The traditional Vietnamese recipe calls for roast pork and shrimp, but chicken breast, cooked fish or surimi crab meat may be substituted instead.

Rice vermicelli, Vietnamese fish sauce, Oriental mint and rice paper, known as banh trang, are available in Oriental markets. Cilantro is also available in Oriental markets, Latin American markets and most grocery stores.

Nutrition information per serving: calories, 230; fat, 1.6 grams; carbohydrate, 33.7 grams; cholesterol, 55 milligrams; sodium, 582 milligrams.

Nuoc Leo

¼ cup hoisin sauce
1 tablespoon fish sauce
3 tablespoons hot water
2 tablespoons dry-roasted, unsalted peanuts, ground
1 teaspoon Oriental chili sauce (optional)

Combine all ingredients. Stir well to blend. Divide into individual bowls to serve.

Makes a little more than ½ cup or about 8 servings.

Test kitchen notes: Hoisin sauce is available in most supermarkets and in Oriental groceries. It is commonly served in Vietnamese restaurants.

Nutrition information per tablespoon without Oriental chili sauce (values will vary depending on how much sauce adheres to food): calories, 20.3; fat, 1.3 grams; carbohydrate, 1.3 grams; cholesterol, 0 milligrams; sodium, 518 milligrams.

■ Fresh tortellini are sold in the refrigerated foods section of most grocery stores. Arrange on long bamboo skewers for an attractive party appetizer.

Tortellini With Pesto Dipping Sauce

1 pound fresh spinach or egg tortellini stuffed with cheese

3 tablespoons balsamic vinegar, divided

2 tablespoons olive oil

6 cloves garlic

1 ounce walnuts (about ¼ cup)

3 to 4 cups fresh basil leaves, clean and dry

⅓ cup freshly grated Parmesan cheese

3 tablespoons chicken broth

1 tablespoon cholesterol-free mayonnaise

Bring 2 quarts of salted water to a rolling boil. Add tortellini and cook according to package instructions, about 4 to 5 minutes. Drain and rinse with warm water. In a large bowl, toss with about half the balsamic vinegar.

Meanwhile, combine the olive oil and garlic in the bowl of a food processor or blender and puree. Add the nuts, basil, cheese and process to a fine paste. With motor running, add chicken broth and remaining balsamic vinegar. Stir in cholesterol-free mayonnaise.

To serve as an appetizer, thread 2 to 3 tortellini on long bamboo skewers. Serve warm or at room temperature with pesto dipping sauce. Alternately, toss the pesto with the tortellini and serve as a first course garnished with chopped basil or parsley.

Makes 10 appetizer servings or 6 first-course servings.

Nutrition information per appetizer serving: calories, 178; fat, 8.3 grams; carbohydrate, 20.3 grams; cholesterol, 17 milligrams; sodium, 152 milligrams.

13

■ This light version of a traditional Middle Eastern dish is time-consuming to prepare. Make a big batch because dolmas stay fresh for several days in the refrigerator and they freeze well.

Greek Dolmas (Stuffed Grape Leaves)

1 (8-ounce) jar of grape leaves, drained
2 tablespoons olive oil
1 large onion, finely chopped
1 cup uncooked short-grain rice
¼ cup minced fresh parsley
2 tablespoons chopped fresh dill
2 tablespoons fresh mint, chopped, or
½ teaspoon dried and crushed
1 tomato, seeded and finely chopped
3 tablespoons currants or raisins
1 cup water
⅓ cup pine nuts, toasted
6 tablespoons lemon juice
2 cups defatted, low-sodium beef broth
Lemon wedges

Rinse grape leaves in cold, running water; drain well. Remove stems with a small, sharp knife.

Heat 2 tablespoons of the olive oil in a skillet; add onion. Saute over medium heat until lightly browned (about 4 to 5 minutes). Add rice, parsley, dill, mint, tomato and currants or raisins and 1 cup of water. Cover and reduce heat. Simmer until liquid is absorbed; cool. Stir in pine nuts.

Place 1 teaspoon of rice mixture in center of each leaf, shiny surface down. Fold sides of grape leaf to center and fold the bottom of the leaf over the filling. Then roll up leaf loosely to allow rice to expand.

Step 1: Remove grape leaves from jar and rinse in cold running water to separate them. Drain water and place the individual leaves on a clean work surface. Place grape leaf, vein side up, with the stem toward you. Cut stem end off at the leaf line.

Preheat oven to 350 F.

Arrange rolls in layers in a large baking dish. Sprinkle with lemon juice. In a separate saucepan, bring beef broth to a boil. Pour mixture over rolls. Weight rolls down with a baking dish to keep in place; cover. Simmer in oven for 35 minutes or until firm to the touch; cool. To serve, arrange on a platter and garnish with lemon wedges.

Makes 48 appetizer servings.

Nutrition information per serving of stuffing: calories, 31; fat, 1.2 grams; carbohydrate, 4.6 grams; cholesterol, 0 milligrams; sodium, 1 milligrams.

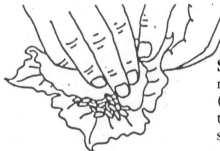

Step 2: Put a mound of stuffing mixture in the middle of the leaf (about 1 teaspoon to 1 tablespoon, depending on the size of the leaf).

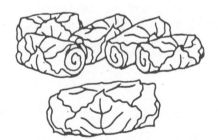

Step 3: Fold in sides of leaf over the mixture and roll up leaf.

Step 4: Layer rolled leaves close together in a large pan. Add beef broth to cover the grape leaves. Press them down with a heavy heatproof plate that fits inside the pan. Cover and bake for 35 minutes. Remove from pan with tongs and let cool until serving time.

15

■ Artichokes filled with salmon mousse are an attractive combination of flavors and pastel colors. Serve them for a warm-weather luncheon.

Braised Artichokes With Salmon Mousse

8 artichokes, each about 2 inches
   in diameter
2 green onions, chopped
½ cup defatted chicken broth
¼ cup red-wine vinegar
1 tablespoon good-quality
   prepared mustard
⅛ teaspoon salt
⅛ teaspoon sugar

Use kitchen shears to trim tops of artichokes and to snip off tops of leaves. Pull off and discard all tough, exterior leaves. Slice off stems. Cut artichokes in half lengthwise.

In a microwave-safe baking dish, combine the green onions, chicken broth, vinegar, mustard, salt and sugar. Place artichokes in dish, cut-side down. Cover and cook in a microwave oven on high (100 percent) power for 6 minutes. Turn artichokes over and spoon some of the cooking liquid over the top. Cover and cook 6 minutes longer on high. Continue basting with cooking liquid, and turning at 3-minute intervals until artichokes are done, about 18 minutes. (Cooking times will vary according to size of vegetable and power of microwave oven. Cooking times will also be shorter if fewer artichokes are cooked at a time.)

Artichokes are done when a center leaf pulls out easily.

Use a spoon to remove the fuzzy choke from center of each cooked artichoke. Fill the cavity with Salmon Mousse (recipe

How to prepare artichokes for other types of cooking

Step 1: Cut off stems and top 2 inches of artichokes; discard. Trim the outer dark green layer from the artichoke bottoms. Cut artichokes in half lengthwise.

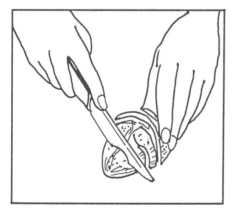

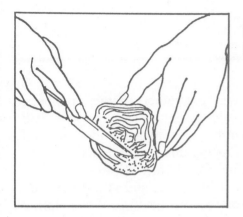

Step 2: Cut out center petals and fuzzy centers (left).

Step 3: Vertically slice each artichoke half to the desired thickness.

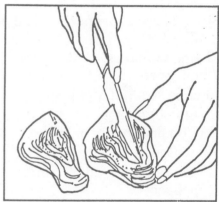

follows). Chill well.
    Makes 4 servings.

    Nutrition information per 2-artichoke serving without mousse: calories, 140; fat, 0.7 gram; carbohydrate, 31.5 grams; cholesterol, 0 milligrams; sodium, 321 milligrams.

Salmon Mousse

½ pound fresh salmon, cooked and chilled
½ cup low-fat cottage cheese
2 tablespoons fresh lemon or lime juice
½ teaspoon dried dill or 1 tablespoon fresh dill
1 teaspoon tomato paste
4 teaspoons capers, drained

    In the bowl of a blender or food processor, combine salmon, cottage cheese, lemon or lime juice, dill and tomato paste. Puree until smooth. Stir in capers. Spoon mousse into halved artichokes. Serve 2 halves per person.
    Makes 8 servings.
    Test kitchen notes: Smoked, boned mullet or smoked salmon may be used in place of fresh salmon. One (16-ounce) can of salmon also can be substituted.

    Nutrition information per serving: calories, 76; fat, 3.4 grams; carbohydrate, 1.1 grams; cholesterol, 26 milligrams; sodium, 188 milligrams.

■ This is the perfect soup for using up a bounty of Florida vegetables. Sherry gives this low-sodium version a special flavor.

Chilled Gazpacho

1 cucumber, peeled, seeded and chopped

1 clove garlic

1 small red pepper, seeded and diced

1 small green pepper, seeded and diced

2 ripe tomatoes, seeded and chopped

3 cups No-Salt V-8 juice or tomato juice

¼ cup dry sherry or white wine

½ teaspoon salt

¼ teaspoon freshly ground pepper

1 tablespoon Worcestershire sauce

1 tablespoon fresh lemon or lime juice

4 tablespoons non-fat yogurt, for garnish

4 tablespoons freshly chopped cilantro or parsley, for garnish

Combine cucumber, garlic, peppers, tomatoes, juice, sherry, salt, pepper and Worcestershire sauce in a blender or food processor. Process until ingredients are juicy but still slightly chunky. Season to taste with lemon or lime juice and salt, if desired.

Refrigerate until ready to serve. Before serving, top each portion with non-fat yogurt and sprinkle with chopped cilantro or parsley.

Makes 4 servings.

Test kitchen notes: This soup is best if made ahead so flavors have a chance to meld. The soup will keep for up to a week in a tightly sealed container in the refrigerator or for a longer period in the freezer.

Nutrition information per serving: calories, 85; fat, 0.5 gram; carbohydrate, 17.3 grams; cholesterol, 0 milligrams; sodium, 349 milligrams.

■ Look for Florida sweet corn to make this summery soup. With a salad, it makes a full meal.

Grilled Corn Chowder With Clams

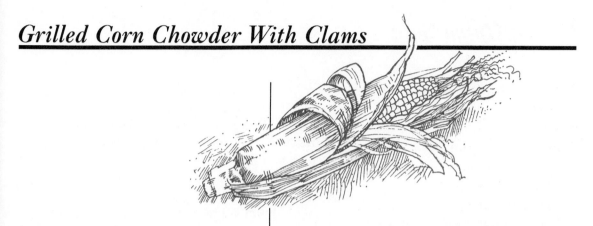

4 ears sweet corn, unshucked
1 tablespoon olive oil
1 tablespoon flour
¼ teaspoon white pepper
Pinch nutmeg
½ teaspoon sugar
4 cups chicken broth
1 small onion, minced
1 clove garlic, minced
¼ cup buttermilk (1 percent fat)
6 ounces canned or fresh-
  shucked baby clams, with juice
¼ cup sherry
4 tablespoons fresh parsley,
  minced

Soak the ears of corn in cold water for 15 minutes to thoroughly wet the husks. Trim away corn silk. Barbecue corn on a grill over medium-high coals for 15 to 20 minutes until husks are slightly charred. Do not allow the husks to catch on fire. Remove from heat and allow to cool. When cool enough to handle, shuck the corn and scrape the kernels off with a sharp knife. Scrape again with the dull side of the knife to remove the creamy inside portions; set aside.

In a large saucepan or kettle, heat olive oil over medium-high heat. Whisk in the flour, white pepper and nutmeg. Cook for 1 minute, until flour adheres to bottom and sides of pan. Add the chicken broth slowly, stirring until mixture comes to a boil and thickens slightly. Add the onion, garlic and corn; simmer for 15 to 20 minutes. Stir in the buttermilk, clams and sherry. Heat thoroughly. Divide into 4 portions and garnish with parsley.

Makes 4 servings.

Nutrition information per serving: calories, 213; fat, 5.9 grams; carbohydrate, 25.2 grams; cholesterol, 19 milligrams; sodium, 444 milligrams.

■ If you are lucky enough to find Florida sweet onions in the spring, you will love the delicate flavor they add to soup.

French Onion Soup

2 (8- to 10-ounce) medium sweet Spanish or Vidalia onions
¼ cup olive oil
2 tablespoons flour
2 (10½-ounce) cans condensed beef bouillon
2½ cups water
6 slices French bread, cut 1-inch thick
2 ounces grated Parmesan cheese
2 ounces grated Swiss cheese

Peel and slice onions. Saute onion rings in oil until soft. Stir in flour, bouillon and water. Bring to a boil stirring constantly. Reduce heat and simmer 20 minutes. Toast bread. Place in 6 oven-proof bowls. Add soup. Top with cheese. Bake at 425 F for 10 minutes.

Makes 6 servings.

Nutrition information per serving: calories, 296; fat, 15.2 grams; carbohydrate, 25.1 grams; cholesterol, 37 milligrams; sodium, 994 milligrams.

■ Once you discover this colorful, swirled soup, you may keep a batch in your freezer for a rainy day.

Two-Toned Soup
(Creamy Cauliflower With a Red Pepper Swirl)

2 leeks or 2 Vidalia or Florida
    sweet onions
1 tablespoon olive oil
3 cups cauliflower florets (about
    1 head)
1 potato, peeled and diced
½ teaspoon salt
1 bay leaf
2 cups skim milk
2 cups chicken stock or water

Rinse the leeks thoroughly; trim ends and green tops. Slice cleaned leeks thinly. (If using Vidalia onions, trim root end. Slice and include some of the tender green stem end.)

Heat the olive oil in a large kettle. Saute the leeks or onions over medium-high heat for 5 to 7 minutes, stirring frequently, until soft. Add the cauliflower, potato, salt, bay leaf, milk and chicken stock or water.

Bring mixture to a boil. Reduce heat and simmer for 20 minutes. When vegetables are tender, use a slotted spoon to remove vegetables from liquid and place them in the bowl of a food processor or blender. Process until smooth, adding a small amount of cooking liquid if necessary to make a smooth puree. Return vegetables to kettle. Simmer for 10 minutes longer. Keep warm.

While soup is cooking, follow instructions to make the red pepper swirl.

Swirl 2 tablespoons of the red pepper puree into each serving of the soup.

Makes 4 servings.

Ways to reduce fat and cholesterol from dairy products:
■ Switch from whole milk to skim milk.
■ Use low-fat, skim milk cheeses such as mozzarella, ricotta or cottage cheese in place of aged cheeses.
■ Avoid frequent use of half-and-half, cream or evaporated milk.
■ Use evaporated skimmed milk in cooking.
■ Avoid using butter.
■ Limit your use of cream cheese.

Test kitchen notes: This cold-weather soup also can be made with broccoli in place of the cauliflower. Follow the same recipe and instructions but substitute broccoli. Swirl the broccoli soup with a puree made of yellow peppers instead of red. The soup can be frozen for up to 3 months or kept refrigerated tightly covered for 3 days.

Serve with warm crusty, whole grain rolls and a green salad.

Nutrition information per serving: calories, 129; fat, 5.6 grams; carbohydrate, 14.1 grams; cholesterol, 2 milligrams; sodium, 869 milligrams.

Red Pepper Swirl

2 medium red peppers
1 clove garlic
¼ teaspoon salt
1 teaspoon lemon juice

Pierce peppers with a knife. Cook over a hot grill until the skins are charred. Or split peppers in half and char skins under an oven broiler. Put charred peppers into a paper or heavy-duty plastic bag. Peppers will steam inside bag as they cool. After about 10 minutes, or until they are cool enough to handle, peel and seed vegetables. Reserve as much juice as possible. Combine pepper flesh with garlic, salt and lemon juice in the bowl of a food processor or blender. Puree mixture. If desired, strain sauce through a sieve before serving.

Makes 1 cup.

Test kitchen notes: The puree can be frozen or stored covered in the refrigerator for up to a week.

Nutrition information per serving: calories, 26; fat, 0.4 gram; carbohydrate, 5.5 grams; cholesterol, 0 milligrams; sodium, 3 milligrams.

SALADS

■ Americans are finally discovering that sweet potatoes do not have to be drenched in butter, sugar and marshmallows to taste good. In this recipe, onion and honey heighten the natural flavor.

Sweet Potato Salad

3½ pounds sweet potatoes
  (about 4 large)
1 medium onion, cut into thin
  rings
1 green pepper, cut into thin
  strips
Honey Vinaigrette Dressing
  (recipe follows)

Wash sweet potatoes.

Pierce each with a knife. Place in a covered microwave baking dish. Microwave for 8 minutes on high (100 percent) power. Turn potatoes over and cook for another 8 minutes. Allow to stand for 4 minutes. Potatoes should be soft to the touch but not shriveled. If still too hard, cook for 4 minutes longer. (Unpeeled potatoes can be cooked on the stovetop in boiling water for 20 minutes until just fork tender.)

When cool enough to handle, peel potatoes and halve lengthwise. Cut into ¼-inch slices. Combine sweet potato slices, onion rings and green pepper strips in large bowl. Pour Honey Vinaigrette Dressing over salad mixture. Toss lightly to coat vegetables.

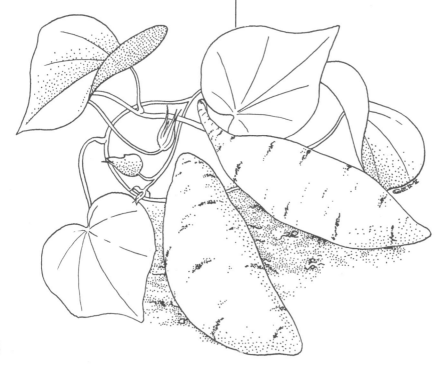

Cover and refrigerate 3 to 6 hours or overnight. Serve chilled or at room temperature.

Makes 8 servings.

Test kitchen note: This colorful salad is best when made a day in advance, allowing the sweet potato slices to absorb the tart vinaigrette dressing.

Nutrition information per serving without Honey Vinaigrette Dressing: calories, 98; fat, 0.4 gram; carbohydrate, 22.5 grams; cholesterol, 0 milligrams; sodium, 12 milligrams.

Honey Vinaigrette Dressing

½ cup tarragon vinegar
¼ cup olive oil
1 tablespoon honey
2 cloves garlic, crushed through
   a press
2 bay leaves
½ teaspoon salt
¼ teaspoon pepper
¼ teaspoon oregano
¼ teaspoon thyme

Combine all ingredients in jar with a tightfitting lid.

Shake vigorously until mixed well. Let flavors meld for a few hours. Remove bay leaves before serving.

Nutrition information per serving for entire preparation (values will vary depending on how much dressing adheres to food): calories, 344; sodium, 168 milligrams; fat, 14 grams; carbohydrate, 53.1 grams.

Sweet potatoes

■ Sweet potatoes may look funny but they are one of nature's most beautiful foods. They are high in vitamin A, potassium, calcium and fiber yet contain almost no fat or sodium.

■ Sweet potatoes are naturally sweet so they don't require additional sugar or butter to make them taste good.

■ These vegetables can be cooked in the same manner as white potatoes. They can be eaten raw, baked, grilled over coals, boiled, mashed, sliced for oven-fries or diced for hash-browns. They can be grated for potato pancakes or sliced and steamed for vegetable trays, too.

■ More of the vitamins and minerals are retained when sweet potatoes are cooked in their skins. The cooked skins are a great source of natural fiber.

■ Sweet potatoes are excellent cooked in the microwave oven. Pierce the skin with a knife or fork and microwave until the surface is soft, about 5 minutes per potato. Allow to stand for 5 minutes longer before serving.

■ Beautiful colors and refreshing flavors make this salad a hit at picnics and family gatherings. Be sure to use ripe strawberries.

Strawberry-Avocado Salad

3 cups spinach leaves, torn in bite-size pieces

1 cup green or red seedless grapes, sliced in half

2 oranges, peeled and sectioned

2 cups whole fresh strawberries, washed, hulled and sliced in half

2 avocados, seeded, peeled and cubed

¼ cup chopped pecans

Dressing:

1 cup low-fat strawberry yogurt

1 teaspoon fresh dill or ½ teaspoon dried

Place the spinach leaves in the bottom of a large salad bowl. Arrange the fruit and avocados on top. Sprinkle with pecans.

To prepare the dressing, stir the dill into the yogurt and serve on the side in a small bowl.

Makes 6 servings.

Nutrition information per serving: calories, 244; fat, 14.5 grams; carbohydrate, 28.3 grams; cholesterol, 4 milligrams; sodium, 71 milligrams.

Fast facts

Florida's harvest kicks off the strawberry season.

In Plant City, the Winter Strawberry Capital of the World, growers celebrate the peak of the harvest during March with the Florida Strawberry Festival. Berries have been the star of the Hillsborough County Fair since the 1930s.

How to prepare avocados

Step 1: Cut avocado lengthwise around the seed; twist gently to separate halves.

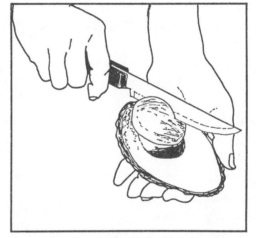

Step 2: To remove seed, strike it with a blade of a sharp knife so the blade lodges in seed; twist knife gently to lift out seed.

Step 3: Peel and slice or cut up, depending on use. Or use unpeeled as a shell for salads or filling. To prevent browning, sprinkle with lemon juice.

■ The great colors in this salad make it look like an art deco creation. It tastes as good as it looks and it is a great source of soluble fiber and complex carbohydrates.

Black and White Salad

7 ounces dried black beans

7 ounces dried white Great Northern beans

3 cloves garlic

½ cup finely minced green onions (about 2)

¼ cup fresh cilantro, parsley or other herb

1 cup red pepper, chopped

2 tomatoes, seeded and chopped

1 cup green or yellow pepper, chopped

3 tablespoons apple-cider or red-wine vinegar

2 tablespoons chicken broth

1 tablespoon extra-virgin olive oil

1 teaspoon salt

¼ teaspoon freshly ground black pepper

Wash beans separately. Put in separate kettles and cover with water. Bring both kettles to a boil. Cook 5 minutes. Remove from heat and allow to stand in water 1 hour.

Drain beans separately. Return to separate kettles. Cover with water 3 inches above top of beans. Add 1 whole clove of garlic to each kettle. Bring to a boil and cook for 1 hour, or until beans are tender.

Drain and allow to cool to room temperature. Finely mince remaining clove of garlic. Combine minced garlic, green onions, cilantro or other fresh herb, chopped peppers, and tomatoes in a large bowl.

When beans are cool, toss with vegetable mix. In a jar, combine vinegar, broth, olive oil, salt and pepper. Shake vigorously to blend. Pour dressing over salad and toss to blend.

Allow salad to stand for at least 30 minutes to blend flavors.

Makes 8 servings.

Test kitchen notes: Bringing the beans to a boil and allowing them to stand for 1 hour, eliminates the need to pre-soak the beans overnight. Cooking the beans separately keeps the colors distinct and attractive. This hearty summer salad would pair well with a warm carrot soup or light seafood broth.

If the salad absorbs the dressing, add 2 more tablespoons of chicken broth and 2 more tablespoons of vinegar.

Nutrition information per serving: calories, 205; fat, 2.6 grams; carbohydrate, 35.9 grams; cholesterol, 0 milligrams; sodium, 318 milligrams.

■ The smoky flavor of lentils contrasts wonderfully with the salty tang of feta cheese and the refreshing crunch of cucumbers. The lentils are ready to eat in just 15 minutes.

Mediterranean Lentil Salad

2 cups lentils

4 cups water

3 cloves garlic, minced

1 teaspoon salt

1 cup tomatoes, seeded and chopped

1 cup cucumbers, peeled, seeded and chopped

½ cup parsley, finely chopped

2 green onions, finely chopped

1 teaspoon capers, rinsed in cold water and drained

3 tablespoons red-wine vinegar

¼ cup plus 1 teaspoon extra-virgin olive oil

¼ teaspoon freshly ground black pepper

3 tablespoons chopped fresh basil or oregano or 1 teaspoon dried

4 ounces feta cheese crumbled

4 whole wheat pita breads

4 leaves Boston or romaine lettuce

Lemon wedges

Wash lentils and discard any that float or that may be moldy. Combine lentils, water, garlic and ½ teaspoon of the salt in a kettle and bring to a boil; reduce heat. Cover and simmer for 15 minutes or until lentils are just tender. Do not overcook, or lentils will become mushy. Drain and allow to cool to room temperature.

Combine cooled lentils with tomatoes, cucumbers, parsley, green onions, capers, ¼ cup of olive oil, vinegar, remaining ½ teaspoon salt, pepper, basil or oregano and feta cheese. Toss to mix well. Chill if desired.

Preheat oven to 325 F. Brush pita breads with remaining 1 teaspoon olive oil. Toast breads until crisp, about 10 to 12 minutes. Remove from heat. Line the pita breads with lettuce. Fill each with lentil salad and garnish with lemon wedges.

Makes 4 servings.

Test kitchen note: Lentils can be prepared a day in advance and allowed to chill. The vegetables can be prepared several hours in advance.

Nutrition information per serving: calories, 409; fat, 22.1 grams; carbohydrate, 41.7 grams; cholesterol, 25 milligrams; sodium, 620 milligrams.

■ Think of this as a Chinese-style warm salad. The crunchy lettuce is slightly wilted by the tangy sauce.

Beef and Tomato Stir-Fry Salad

Put chopstick between thumb and first finger. This chopstick will be stationary when using.

1 pound lean, boneless tender beef
1 tablespoon cornstarch
4 tablespoons soy sauce, divided
½ teaspoon sugar
1 clove garlic, minced
1 tablespoon red-wine vinegar
1 tablespoon low-sodium ketchup
3 tablespoons vegetable oil, divided
1 teaspoon onion powder
4 cups shredded iceberg lettuce
2 stalks celery, cut diagonally into ¼-inch slices
1 green pepper, julienned
2 teaspoons minced fresh ginger
15 cherry tomatoes, halved

The upper chopstick is positioned between the same fingers only a little higher than the first. Keeping the bottom stick stationary, press the top stick down so that they meet at the points.

Cut beef into thin strips. Combine cornstarch, 2 tablespoons soy sauce, sugar and garlic; stir in beef. Marinate 15 minutes. Meanwhile, combine remaining soy sauce with vinegar, ketchup, 1 tablespoon oil, onion powder and 2 tablespoons water; set aside.

Arrange lettuce to line large shallow bowl or large platter. Heat 1 tablespoon oil in hot wok or large skillet over high heat. Add beef and stir-fry for 1 minute; remove. Heat remaining oil in the same wok. Add celery, green pepper and ginger; stir-fry for 1 minute.

Remove wok from heat; stir in tomatoes, beef and soy sauce mixture. Spoon mixture over lettuce; toss well to combine before serving. Serve immediately.

Makes 6 servings.

Nutrition information per serving: calories, 201; fat, 10.8 grams; carbohydrate, 7.6 grams; cholesterol, 39 milligrams; sodium, 609 milligrams.

■ The combination of feathery napa or celery cabbage, nutty sesame seeds and crunchy snow peas gives this colorful salad a range of delightful textures.

Chinese Coleslaw

1 head napa cabbage
½ head green cabbage
1 red pepper
¼ pound snow peas
1 handful fresh bean sprouts
1 tablespoon sesame seeds,
  toasted
Sesame Ginger Dressing (recipe
  150)

Separate the napa cabbage leaves and discard the central core. Cut out the stems from the leaves. Dice the stems finely and slice the leaves into narrow strips. Shred the green cabbage into thin strips. Combine with the napa cabbage.

Cut off top and bottom of the red pepper. Remove the seeds and pith from the inside of the ring. Cut through and lay out flat. Slice into narrow julienne strips about 2 inches long.

Remove stem end of the snow peas and slice lengthwise into narrow strips. Add the bean sprouts and sesame seeds. Toss. Refrigerate until ready to dress.

Makes 4 servings.

Nutrition information per serving without dressing (values will vary depending on size of vegetables used): calories, 77; fat, 1.8 grams; carbohydrate, 13.3 grams; cholesterol, 0 milligrams; sodium, 115 milligrams.

If you have a mint patch in your back yard, you may enjoy this light, refreshing salad all summer long. Mint is also sold in Oriental markets and many grocery stores.

Mint Coleslaw

1 head green cabbage
1 bunch fresh mint leaves, finely chopped (or ½ teaspoon dried mint, crushed)
1 cucumber, peeled, seeded and diced
3 inches of daikon radish, peeled and diced (or 7 red radishes, chopped)
1 cup frozen green peas, thawed
Mint Vinaigrette (recipe follows)

Shred the green cabbage. Combine with the chopped mint, cucumber, radish and peas. Refrigerate until ready to serve. Toss with dressing before serving.

Makes 8 servings.

Nutrition information per serving without vinaigrette: calories, 47; fat, 0.2 gram; carbohydrate, 9.7 grams; cholesterol, 0 milligrams; sodium, 44 milligrams.

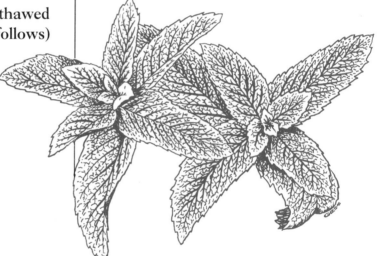

Mint Vinaigrette

¼ cup mint vinegar (or cider vinegar)
3 tablespoons canola oil
¼ teaspoon dried mint, crushed
¼ teaspoon salt
¼ cup non-fat plain yogurt
¼ teaspoon sugar
2 tablespoons cholesterol-free mayonnaise

Combine all ingredients and shake to blend. Refrigerate until ready to serve.

Makes 8 servings.

Nutrition information per serving: calories, 62; fat, 6.5 grams; carbohydrate, 1.1 grams; cholesterol, 2 milligrams; sodium, 99 milligrams.

■Magenta red cabbage, orange carrot gratings and yellow corn kernels make this salad an impressive presentation for any occasion. However, do not toss the mixture in advance because the red cabbage stains the other vegetables.

Mardi Gras Slaw

1 head red cabbage
1½ cups sweet corn, fresh, canned or frozen
2 carrots, peeled and grated (about 1½ to 2 cups)
1 large tart, green apple, cored and finely diced
Creamy Pineapple Dressing (recipe 151)

Shred red cabbage. Combine with corn, carrots and apples. Toss and refrigerate until ready to dress.

Makes 8 servings.

Nutrition information per serving: calories, 50; fat, 0.2 gram; carbohydrate, 12.3 grams; cholesterol, 0 milligrams; sodium, 11 milligrams.

■ A combination of fresh, canned and frozen vegetables paired with toasted nuts and piquant red-wine vinegar make this salad a year-round crowd-pleaser.

Tossed Vegetables With Pecan Dressing

8 small red-skinned potatoes, sliced into ½-inch pieces

½ pound green beans, trimmed and sliced into ½-inch pieces

1-pound can wax beans, drained

1½ cups corn, canned or frozen

1 small cucumber, peeled and sliced

2 cups halved cherry tomatoes

¾ cup celery, sliced into ½-inch pieces

1 small onion, sliced and separated into rings

⅓ cup red-wine vinegar

¼ cup olive oil

3 tablespoons chopped toasted pecans

½ teaspoon salt

⅛ teaspoon pepper

Cook sliced potatoes in boiling salted water for 10 minutes. Remove from boiling water with a slotted spoon and allow to drain. Add green beans to water and cook 7 minutes. Add canned beans and corn and cook 3 minutes. Drain and rinse in ice water. Drain and combine in a bowl with cucumber, cherry tomatoes, celery and onion. Combine vinegar, oil, pecans, salt and pepper; stir. Pour mixture over vegetables. Serve immediately at room temperature.

Makes 6 servings.

Nutrition information per serving: calories, 324; fat, 10.1 grams; carbohydrate, 54.5 grams; cholesterol, 0 milligrams; sodium, 463 milligrams.

Fast facts

To reduce the risks of heart disease, physicians recommend these measures:

Exercise.

Quit smoking.

Keep blood pressure under control.

Eat less saturated fat and high-cholesterol foods.

Maintain a healthy body weight.

Eat more high-fiber foods.

■ Do not be worried about the number of ingredients in this salad — it is simple and fast to make. The nuts, peas and chickpeas give the feather-light couscous a crunchy texture.

Curried Shrimp and Couscous Salad

1 tablespoon olive oil

1 cup quick-cooking couscous

½ teaspoon salt

1 tablespoon curry powder

¼ teaspoon cinnamon

½ teaspoon cumin

1 teaspoon freshly grated orange rind

¼ cup raisins

2 green onions, finely chopped

1½ cups defatted chicken broth

½ cup frozen green peas, thawed

½ cup frozen corn, thawed

½ cup cooked chickpeas, drained

½ cup slivered almonds, toasted

2 tablespoons fresh orange juice

1 orange, sectioned

¼ cup fresh mint or parsley, finely chopped

16 large shrimp, peeled, deveined and cooked

Heat olive oil in large saucepan. Stir in the couscous, coating each grain. Stir in the salt, curry powder, cinnamon, cumin, orange rind, raisins and onions. Add the chicken broth and bring to a boil.

Remove from heat and allow to stand 10 minutes to absorb liquid. Transfer couscous to a large bowl and stir in peas, corn, chickpeas, almonds, orange juice and mint or parsley.

Coat a 5-cup ring mold or souffle dish with non-stick cooking spray. Press couscous mixture into mold. Refrigerate for at least 1 hour or overnight.

When ready to serve, garnish with shrimp and orange segments.

Served with warm pita bread and ripe, sliced tomatoes sprinkled with balsamic vinegar, this salad makes a hearty summer meal.

Makes 4 large servings.

Nutrition information per serving: calories, 375; fat, 16.5 grams; carbohydrate, 36.4 grams; cholesterol, 109 milligrams; sodium, 860 milligrams.

Fast facts

Couscous is a fine pellet, similar to pasta, made from semolina flour. It is available in health-food stores, Middle Eastern markets and in most grocery stores. North African in origin, couscous is gaining popularity with busy cooks because it requires minimal cooking.

■ Hot, sweet and spicy, this exotic salad has enormous appeal. It makes a colorful side dish with Middle Eastern grilled lamb or seafood.

Orange and Black Olive Salad

3 navel or temple oranges
½ cup ripe black olives, pitted
2 tablespoons olive oil
2 cloves garlic, crushed through
  a press
½ teaspoon paprika
⅛ teaspoon cayenne or to taste
¼ teaspoon salt
1 tablespoon honey
Pinch of cumin
2 tablespoons chopped parsley

Peel the oranges and remove the outside membranes using a serrated knife. Section the oranges by cutting away the membranes from the orange flesh. As you work, lift out the orange sections. Arrange the olives and oranges on a serving dish. Make a dressing of the olive oil, garlic, paprika, cayenne, salt, honey and cumin. Pour dressing over the olives and oranges and serve.

Makes 6 servings.

Nutrition information per serving: calories, 96; fat, 5.8 grams; carbohydrate, 1.7 grams; cholesterol, 0 milligrams; sodium, 196 milligrams.

■ Black beans, white rice, red tomatoes — this Cuban-inspired salad is as beautiful as it is flavorful. Serve it for picnics, parties or any time you don't want hot beans and rice.

Caribbean Black Bean and Rice Salad

1 (15-ounce) can of black beans
2 cups cooked rice, chilled (½ cup dry)
1 green pepper, diced
1 medium tomato, seeded and chopped
2 green onions, chopped
3 tablespoons olive oil
2 tablespoons lime juice
½ teaspoon Dijon-style mustard
¼ teaspoon sugar
¼ teaspoon ground cumin
¼ teaspoon ground black pepper
Sprigs of cilantro

Thoroughly drain black beans and discard liquid.

Combine beans with cooked rice, green pepper, tomatoes and green onions. In a separate bowl, combine oil, lime juice, mustard, sugar, cumin and pepper. Beat with a fork to blend. Add dressing to beans and rice and stir gently to coat evenly. Be careful not to crush beans or salad will discolor. Serve chilled.

Makes 6 servings.

Nutrition information per serving: calories, 237; fat, 7.4 grams; carbohydrate, 35.1 grams; cholesterol, 0 milligrams; sodium, 17 milligrams.

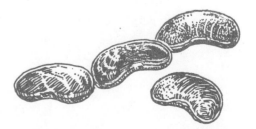

FISH
and shellfish

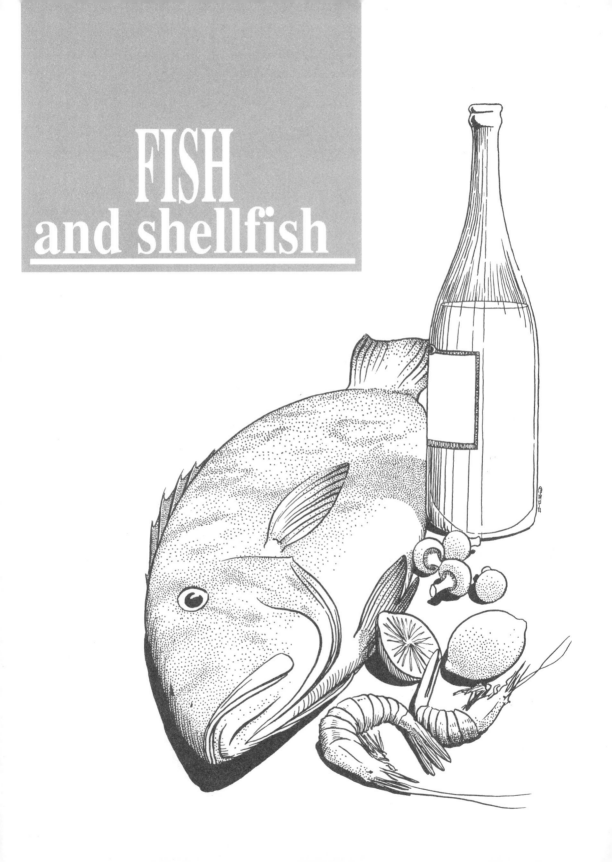

■ Rich and loaded with chunks of salmon and mushrooms, this creamy crepe dish is nutritious and filling.

Salmon in Green Onion and Dill Crepes

Crepes:

¾ cup whole-wheat flour

3 tablespoons cornmeal

2 green onions, finely minced

¼ teaspoon dried dill or 1 tablespoon fresh dill, finely minced

¼ teaspoon salt

1 cup skim milk

2 egg whites

Non-stick cooking spray

Salmon filling:

2 teaspoons olive oil, peanut or canola oil

¼ cup green onions, finely minced

1 tablespoon flour

6 ounces (½ can) evaporated skim milk

1 tablespoon lemon juice

1 tablespoon Dijon-style mustard

¼ teaspoon salt

¼ teaspoon white pepper

¼ teaspoon dried dill or 1 tablespoon fresh dill, finely minced

1 cup sliced, fresh mushrooms

1 pound fresh salmon or 1 (6½-ounce) can salmon packed in water

To make crepes, combine flour, cornmeal, 2 green onions, dill and salt in a blender or food processor. Blend to combine.

Add milk and egg whites and blend until smooth. Batter should have consistency of heavy cream. Refrigerate batter for at least 30 minutes or overnight.

Spray a crepe pan or a 6-inch non-stick skillet with non-stick cooking spray. Pour 2 tablespoons of batter into pan and swirl to coat evenly. Pancakes should be very thin. Repeat and stack pancakes between waxed paper as they are made.

If not using right away, store crepes in an airtight container in the freezer for 1 month or in the refrigerator for 1 week.

Makes 12 crepes.

To make filling, cook mushrooms over medium heat in a non-stick saute pan. Watch carefully and adjust heat to keep from scorching. Set aside.

In a separate saucepan, heat oil over medium heat. Add remaining green onions and cook until soft. Whisk in flour and cook, stirring constantly for 1 minute. Add evaporated skim milk all at once, stirring constantly. Cook until sauce comes to a boil and thickens. Stir in lemon juice, mustard, salt, pepper and dill. Taste for seasonings. Reduce heat to a bare simmer. If sauce seems too thick, add 1 to 3 tablespoons of warm water.

If using fresh salmon, cut into strips about ½ inch wide and 2 inches long. Drop into sauce and cook, without stirring for 5 minutes, or until fish is firm. Stir in mushrooms. If using canned salmon, stir contents into sauce; heat through.

Serve 2 crepes per person. Roll each crepe around ¼ cup of the salmon mixture. Garnish with a little extra sauce and a pinch of dried dill or a sprig of fresh dill.

Makes 4 servings.

Test kitchen notes: Serve with a green salad or green vegetable such as steamed broccoli, snow peas or zucchini. Freeze remaining crepes for another use.

Nutrition information per serving: calories, 372; fat, 10.4 grams; carbohydrate, 32 grams; cholesterol, 48 milligrams; sodium, 566 milligrams.

How to make crepes

Step 1: In a medium bowl, mix crepe ingredients. Cover and refrigerate batter at least 30 minutes or overnight.

Step 2: Brush bottom of small skillet or crepe pan with butter or coat with non-stick cooking spray.

Step 3: Pour 2 tablespoons of batter into heated pan; tip pan to coat with batter. Cook until top is set and underside is just browned. Crepes will be very thin.

Step 4: With a metal spatula, lift the edge of the crepe all around. Shake pan gently so crepe will come loose.

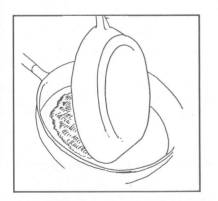

Step 5: Invert crepe onto a warming pan and repeat procedure with remaining batter.

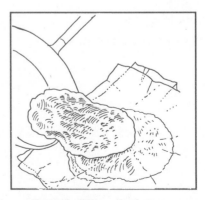

Step 6: Slip cooked crepe onto wax paper. Stack crepes one on top of another to keep warm.

■ This fast and easy sauce complements fresh tuna and pasta without adding extra fat. Canned water-packed tuna may be substituted for fresh.

Pasta With Fresh Tuna and Fresh Tomato Sauce

Drug therapy may be required as a treatment for high cholesterol in individuals who have a family history of heart disease or who already have symptoms of heart disease. For the majority of Americans, eating a low-cholesterol diet, exercising and maintaining an ideal weight are the only measures needed to reduce cholesterol levels.

1 teaspoon olive oil
2 tablespoons Marsala wine or cooking sherry
3 cloves garlic, coarsely chopped
1 small onion, minced
5 large ripe tomatoes, peeled, seeded and coarsely chopped
1 tablespoon tomato paste
¼ teaspoon freshly grated nutmeg
¼ teaspoon salt
1 pound fresh tuna, cut into ¼-inch chunks or 1 (6.5-ounce) can tuna packed in water
1 teaspoon salt
Non-stick cooking spray
1 pound rigatoni or penne pasta

Have all ingredients at hand before starting to cook. In a saucepan, heat oil over medium-high heat. Add garlic and cook just until it begins to brown, about 30 seconds. Immediately add Marsala or cooking sherry and onion. Stir in tomatoes, tomato paste, fresh nutmeg and salt and cook for 10 minutes. Add tuna chunks and cook without stirring for 5 minutes longer. Do not overcook. Remove from heat and set aside.

Bring a large kettle of water to a boil. Add 1 teaspoon salt and spray the surface of the water with non-stick cooking spray. Cook rigatoni or penne pasta until tender but not mushy, about 10 minutes. Drain. Stir in a ladle full of sauce and toss to coat.

Spoon pasta onto individual plates and top with remaining sauce. If desired, garnish with fresh basil, sliced into strands.

Makes 4 hearty servings.

Test kitchen notes: Serve with a fresh green salad, bread sticks and lemon sorbet for dessert.

Nutrition information per serving: calories, 244; fat, 2.3 grams; carbohydrate, 35.2 grams; cholesterol, 0 milligrams; sodium, 656 milligrams.

■ Fresh tuna is firm and meaty. It makes this elegant, French-inspired salad a full meal in itself.

Fresh Tuna Salade Nicoise

2 (8- to 10-ounce) tuna steaks
1 tablespoon lemon juice
1 small head romaine lettuce or two heads Boston lettuce
2 cups green beans, cut into 2-inch pieces
½ cup water
¼ teaspoon salt
2 cups red-skin potatoes, cut into ¼-inch slices
8 black olives, preferably Nicoise or Kalamata
4 fresh anchovy fillets
1 cup Tomato-Basil Vinaigrette (recipe follows)

Arrange tuna in a shallow glass dish. Rub with lemon juice. Cook tuna over an outdoor grill until just firm to the touch, about 12 to 14 minutes. (Tuna is best if cooked to medium-rare stage.) Tuna may be cooked in a microwave oven on high (100 percent) until firm to the touch, about 6 minutes. Cool to room temperature.

Tear lettuce into bite-sized pieces and arrange on 4 plates. Refrigerate until ready to assemble salads. Place the green beans in a microwave-safe dish. Add water and salt. Cover with plastic wrap and cook on high power (100 percent) for 3 minutes. Add potatoes to dish. Cover and cook 5 minutes longer, turning once. Refresh under cool water. Drain and allow to cool to room temperature.

When beans and potatoes are cool, flake or slice tuna into pieces. Divide into 4 portions and arrange on lettuce. Arrange beans, potatoes and olives around tuna. Lay 1 anchovy fillet across top.

Pass Tomato-Basil Vinaigrette separately. Serve with warm, whole-grain bread.

Makes 4 servings.

Test kitchen notes: Fresh tuna is frequently available in seafood markets. Low-sodium tuna packed in water may be substituted.

Nutrition information per serving: calories, 347; fat, 9.1 grams; carbohydrate, 26.6 grams; cholesterol, 54 milligrams; sodium, 288 milligrams.

Tomato-Basil Vinaigrette

2 ripe tomatoes, peeled, seeded and
  chopped
1 clove garlic
¼ cup olive oil
4 tablespoons fresh basil, chopped,
  or 1 teaspoon dried basil
¼ cup balsamic vinegar
½ teaspoon sugar
1 tablespoon whole-grain or Dijon-
  style mustard
¼ teaspoon salt
¼ teaspoon freshly ground black
  pepper

Combine all ingredients in a blender or food processor; mix thoroughly. Allow to stand at least 15 minutes for flavors to blend. Serve at room temperature.

Makes 4 servings.

Test kitchen notes: Other fresh herbs, such as parsley, thyme or rosemary can be substituted for basil.

Nutrition information per serving: calories, 143; fat, 13.9 grams; carbohydrate, 4.8 grams; cholesterol, 0 milligrams; sodium, 260 milligrams.

■ Easy and aromatic, this salmon dish can be ready to eat in about 40 minutes. The marinade develops into a shiny glaze as the fish cooks.

Grilled Ginger-Glazed Salmon With Sushi-Rice Pancakes

¼ cup low-sodium soy sauce

¼ cup sherry wine or mirin

2 teaspoons sugar

1 tablespoon fresh ginger, grated

1 clove garlic, crushed

4 fillets of salmon, about 6 ounces each with skin on

Non-stick cooking spray

4 lemon wedges (for garnish)

8 Sushi-Rice Pancakes (recipe follows)

Combine the soy sauce, sherry or mirin, sugar, ginger and garlic in a shallow glass pan. Add salmon and coat with marinade. Marinate fish for 30 minutes. Drain; reserve marinade.

Spray skin side of fish with non-stick spray. Cook over medium-low coals for 10 minutes. Baste with marinade, but do not turn. Halfway through cooking time, close grill and allow to smoke but watch for flare-ups. Allow fish to stand for 3 minutes before serving.

Garnish with lemon. Serve with Sushi-Rice Pancakes.

Makes 4 servings.

Test kitchen notes: Mirin is a sweet, rice wine. It is available at Oriental markets and most major grocery stores. Substitute sherry if necessary.

Nutrition information including Sushi-Rice Pancakes: calories, 556; fat, 21.8 grams; carbohydrate, 48.4 grams; cholesterol, 117 milligrams; sodium, 1,359 milligrams.

Sushi-Rice Pancakes

1 cup short-grain Japanese rice
2 cups water
2 teaspoons salt
4 tablespoons rice vinegar
2 tablespoons sugar
2 tablespoons peanut oil
Non-stick cooking spray

Rinse the rice several times under cold running water. Combine rinsed rice, 2 cups water and salt in a pan. Bring contents to a boil. Reduce heat to low and simmer for 10 minutes, stirring several times to prevent sticking. Turn off heat and allow to steam while covered for another 12 minutes.

Combine rice vinegar and sugar and stir to dissolve sugar. Dump hot rice onto a large flat pan or cookie sheet. Cool rice by fanning it with a paddle or a fan; at the same time toss the rice with a fork or a spatula. While fanning and tossing the rice, sprinkle it with vinegar and sugar mixture.

When rice is cool enough to handle, use wet hands to shape it into cylinders. Or remove the ends from an empty can and pack with rice. Push the rice out of the can with a round flat-bottomed object that is a little smaller than the opening of the can filled with rice. Slice the cylinder of rice into 2-inch rounds.

Pat each slice into a compact pancake.

Turn stove exhaust on high. Spray a non-stick griddle or frying pan with cooking spray. Drizzle with a little peanut oil and cook over medium-high heat until pancakes are golden. Turn and cook on other side until golden brown.

Makes 4 servings.

Test kitchen notes: If you use Oriental short-grain rice, rinse the rice several times in cold water before cooking. Eliminate the rinsing if using American short-grain rice.

Nutrition information per serving: calories, 251; fat, 7 grams; carbohydrate, 44.8 grams; cholesterol, 0 milligrams; sodium, 1,176 milligrams.

■ Simplicity is the beauty of this low-fat entree. It is the perfect light meal for a warm summer evening.

Broiled Halibut or Swordfish With Mint and Lime

Juice of 1 freshly squeezed lime
(or 4 tablespoons)
1 tablespoon olive oil
1 tablespoon soy sauce
1 clove garlic, minced or crushed
through a press
2 tablespoons minced fresh mint
leaves or ½ teaspoon dried
mint
1 pound fresh halibut or
swordfish steaks
1 tablespoon fresh parsley,
minced

Seasonings to substitute for salt and butter

■ Balsamic, rice or fruit-flavored vinegars.
■ Low-sodium soy sauce.
■ Fresh garlic and onion.
■ Garlic or onion powders (not salts).
■ Fresh herbs or herb blends.
■ Salad herbs.
■ Nutmeg, cinnamon or allspice.
■ White wine, red wine, sherry or port.

Combine the lime juice, olive oil, soy, garlic and mint in a shallow dish. Add the fish and marinate 20 minutes to 1 hour, turning several times. Preheat the oven to 425 F. Spoon marinade over the surface of the fish and bake for 12 minutes. Turn oven to broil setting and place rack as close as possible to heat element. Broil fish for 2 minutes. Remove from heat; allow to stand for 1 minute. Divide on warmed plates and spoon marinade over top.

Makes 4 servings.

Test kitchen notes: Other firm-fleshed fish will work in this recipe, such as mahi-mahi (dolphin), shark or grouper. Serve with Chevre-Stuffed Tomatoes (page 135). If desired, the fish can be placed in the marinade in the morning and cooked in the evening.

Nutrition information per serving: calories, 162; fat, 6 grams; carbohydrate, 1.9 grams; cholesterol, 53 milligrams; sodium, 269 milligrams.

■ Rich and remarkably easy to make, this creamy pasta dish would be elegant enough to serve for a dinner party. Tiny, sweet calico scallops from Port Canaveral would be excellent in this dish.

Pasta With Shrimp, Scallops and Saffron

2 tablespoons olive oil
2 cloves garlic
1 tablespoon flour
¼ teaspoon salt
1 cup clam juice (or fish stock)
½ cup evaporated skim milk
⅛ teaspoon saffron
Pinch white pepper
Pinch nutmeg
8 sea scallops, sliced in half
  lengthwise
12 medium shrimp, peeled and
  deveined
1 teaspoon olive oil
1 tablespoon lemon juice
½ cup green peas, fresh or
  frozen and defrosted
1 pound fresh spinach or egg
  linguine or 12 ounces dry

In a saucepan, heat the olive oil over medium heat. Saute the garlic until fragrant, about 30 seconds, then immediately whisk in flour and salt. Cook about 1 minute, until flour adheres slightly to sides and bottom of pan. Slowly whisk in clam juice and evaporated skim milk. Bring mixture to a simmer until thickened. Add nutmeg, saffron and white pepper and simmer 10 minutes longer, stirring occasionally.

Combine scallops and shrimp in a microwave oven-safe dish. Drizzle with olive oil and lemon juice. Cover tightly with microwave-safe plastic wrap and cook on high power (100 percent) in a microwave oven for 2 minutes. Remove from oven and allow to stand 1 minute.

Bring a large kettle of salted water to a boil. Cook linguine according to package directions, 2 minutes for fresh or 7 to 9 minutes for dry. Drain and rinse under warm water.

Divide into 4 portions on warmed dinner plates.

When ready to serve, stir scallops, shrimp and all accumulated cooking juices into the sauce. Add peas and heat through for 1 minute. Spoon sauce and seafood over warm pasta. Serve immediately.

A salad of sliced tomatoes with basil and a slice of crusty Italian bread make a complete dinner.

Makes 4 servings.

Test kitchen notes: Small bay scallops can be used in place of large sea scallops, but allow more per person. Cubed firm-fleshed fish, such as tuna, salmon or halibut may be used instead of shellfish. Adjust cooking time in the microwave oven accordingly.

Nutrition information per serving: calories, 433; fat, 10.7 grams; carbohydrate, 56 grams; cholesterol, 105 milligrams; sodium, 505 milligrams.

> ### *Fast facts*
>
> Evaporated skim milk is a boon to health-conscious cooks. Its thick, velvety texture and creamy taste make it perfect for cooking, yet it has less than 1 gram of fat per cup.

■ Because microwave cooking leaves food so moist, you need little fat to make a delicious and nutritious meal. The almonds are a crunchy counterpoint to the delicate fish.

Sole With Mushrooms, Artichokes and Almonds

2 tablespoons white-wine vinegar

1 tablespoon olive oil

¼ teaspoon dried basil, crumbled

¼ teaspoon ground black pepper

4 sole fillets, about 6 ounces each

Non-stick cooking spray

¼ pound (about 5 large) mushrooms, wiped clean and sliced

4 frozen artichoke hearts, thawed and sliced in half

2 tablespoons sliced almonds

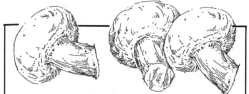

Mushroom tips

■ Never wash or submerge fresh mushrooms in water. Wipe them clean with a damp paper towel.

■ Select mushrooms that are firm and free of soft spots and blemishes.

■ Look for caps that are tightly closed at the stem end. Caps that have sprung open indicate the mushrooms are past peak flavor.

■ Trim stems and chop them for use in recipes where sliced mushrooms are not important.

In a microwave-safe dish, combine vinegar, oil, basil and pepper to make a marinade. Put fish in dish and coat with marinade. Refrigerate for 20 minutes, turning once.

Toast almonds. Remove from heat; cool.

Coat a non-stick skillet with cooking spray. Cook mushrooms until just limp. Add artichokes and cook for 1 minute longer; set aside. Cover fish with waxed paper. Cook on high (100 percent) power in a microwave oven for 2 minutes. Spoon mushrooms and artichokes over top and cook on high for 2 minutes. Sprinkle almonds on top of each fillet. Let stand 3 minutes.

Makes 4 servings.

Nutrition information per serving: calories, 222; fat, 7.4 grams; carbohydrate, 4 grams; cholesterol, 82 milligrams; sodium, 153 milligrams.

■ It is hard to believe a soup so low in fat and cholesterol could be so satisfying. Saffron, tomatoes, fennel seed and orange add zest without adding calories or fat.

Bouillabaisse

2 medium yellow onions, thinly sliced

1 leek, white part only, thinly sliced

2 tablespoons water

2 large cloves garlic

2 (8-ounce) bottles clam juice

1 cup water

1 (15-ounce) can peeled tomatoes, crushed

1 tablespoon orange zest (peel) finely grated

½ cup orange juice, freshly squeezed

⅛ teaspoon saffron threads

1 teaspoon fennel seeds

¼ teaspoon dry thyme, crumbled

¼ pound firm-fleshed fish, such as halibut, tuna, grouper or red snapper

¼ pound delicate-fleshed fish, such as flounder, cod or sole

¼ pound scallops, washed 3 times in cold water

4 large shrimp, peeled and deveined

4 slices Garlic Bread (recipe 167)

Bring the 2 tablespoons of water in a non-aluminum kettle to a gentle boil. Boil the onions and leeks until transparent. Add the garlic and cook for 1 minute longer. Do not allow water to completely boil away.

Add the clam juice, 1 cup of water, tomatoes (including the juice), orange zest, orange juice, saffron, fennel and thyme. Bring broth to a boil and simmer covered for 20 minutes.

Cut the firm-fleshed fish into large cubes, allowing 1 or 2 pieces per person. Cut the delicate fish into strips, allowing 1 or 2 pieces per person. (If the scallops are large, cut them in half.) Remove shrimp from shells and clean.

Five minutes before serving, stir the firm-fleshed fish into the broth. Wait until broth returns to a simmer, then stir in the delicate fish, scallops and shrimp. Simmer for 4 minutes. Remove from heat and ladle seafood and broth into warmed bowls.

Serve each bowl topped with a slice of Garlic Bread.

Makes 4 servings.

Test kitchen notes: The type of fish used depends on personal preference and what is freshest at the fish market or grocery store. However, salmon and oysters are not generally used in bouillabaisse. Whatever fish you select, don't overcook it.

Nutrition information per serving using grouper and sole: calories, 180; fat, 1.7 grams; carbohydrate, 19.3 grams; cholesterol, 61 milligrams; sodium, 379 milligrams.

Fast facts

Shellfish got a reputation as being high in cholesterol from outdated measuring techniques that registered all sterol substances as cholesterol. New measuring techniques have significantly lowered cholesterol values in most shellfish.

However, shellfish — especially crustaceans such as shrimp, crab and lobster — are higher in cholesterol than finfish. For example, 100 grams of Florida blue crab has 78 milligrams of cholesterol while 100 grams of Florida grouper has only 37 milligrams of cholesterol.

That's why the American Heart Association recommends eating shellfish no more than twice weekly.

■ Fresh pasta, dyed ebony-colored with squid ink, is available in many gourmet food shops and grocery stores. It adds a delicate sea-sweetness to the pasta. Other types of fresh pasta can be substituted.

Squid-Ink Pasta
With Fresh Mussels, Garlic and Parsley

1 pound fresh squid-ink pasta (or any fresh pasta)

3 pounds fresh mussels in the shell

4 tablespoons olive oil

2 cloves garlic

½ cup white wine

2 tablespoons chopped fresh parsley

Salt

Freshly ground black pepper to taste

Scrub the mussels and pull off beards, if any.

In a saucepan with a lid, place the mussels, 2 tablespoons of the olive oil and 1 peeled clove garlic in 1 inch of water.

Steam over medium-high heat until all the mussels are open, about 5 minutes. Remove from heat and set pan aside to cool. Strain, reserving the cooking liquid and discarding any mussels that didn't open.

Remove meat from the shells, leaving a few mussels in the shell for decoration. Mince the remaining clove of garlic.

Boil water for cooking the pasta. Cook the fresh pasta for about 1 minute. Drain pasta.

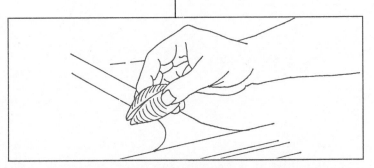

Tap an open mussel gently against the sink or another hard surface; it will close if it is still alive. If a mussel remains open after being tapped, discard it.

In a separate pan, heat the remaining olive oil and saute the garlic in the oil until fragrant. Add the wine and the cooking liquid. Boil for several minutes to reduce some of the liquid, then add mussels. Remove from heat.

Add the pasta to the mussels and stir to coat each strand. Sprinkle with parsley and serve immediately.

Makes 4 servings.

Nutrition information per serving: calories, 617; fat, 22.7 grams; carbohydrate, 69 grams; cholesterol, 48 milligrams; sodium, 470 milligrams.

Fast facts on mussels

■ Mussels are increasingly popular in the United States because they are low in fat and high in iron.

■ An inexpensive ingredient, mussels are readily available in seafood markets and in the frozen food section of most grocery stores.

■ Mussels can cook on the stove in a kettle or deep saucepan in a small amount of liquid in about 5 to 6 minutes. Or, cook in a microwave on high (100 percent) power in about 3 to 4 minutes. No matter what method is used, remove each mussel as it opens to prevent overcooking.

■ The cooking juices of mussels are the only sauce that is needed.

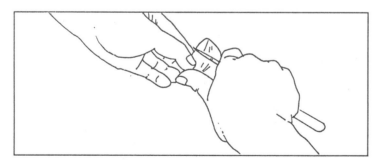

Put the closed shellfish in a colander and rinse them well several times under cold running water. Scrub clams thoroughly with a stiff brush. Scrape mussels with a knife to remove foreign particles that cling to them and the "beard" that joins them together. After mussels are cleaned, their shells should look bright and shiny.

■Almond oil imported from France has the flavor and aroma of lightly toasted almonds. Other types of oil, such as canola, peanut or walnut oil, can also be used.

Grouper Amandine

¼ cup slivered almonds
2 tablespoons chopped parsley
4 green onions, diced
2 tablespoons white wine
2 tablespoons almond oil
1 tablespoon grated fresh lemon rind
2 tablespoons fresh lemon juice
4 grouper fillets

In a large, non-stick skillet, lightly brown the almonds; set aside.

In the same skillet, combine the parsley, green onion, wine, almond oil, lemon rind and lemon juice. Heat until boiling. Allow to boil 3 minutes. Reduce heat to a bare simmer.

Lay the grouper fillets in the poaching liquid, overlapping any very thin pieces. Cover and cook 5 minutes. Regulate heat to keep the liquid simmering but not boiling. Spoon sauce over the fillets. Cook until fillets are opaque and firm to the touch, about 7 to 12 minutes depending on thickness. Using a large spatula, carefully lift fillets to heated plates or a platter.

Bring sauce to a boil and reduce by half. Spoon a small amount of sauce over each fillet. Garnish with toasted almonds.

Makes 4 servings.

Test kitchen notes: Any other firm, mild fish, including halibut, shark, snapper or turbot can substitute for grouper. Almond oil is available in specialty food shops, health food stores and some supermarkets. It has a distinct almond flavor. If a milder flavor is desired, substitute canola or olive oil.

Nutrition information per serving: calories, 319; fat, 16.1 grams; carbohydrate, 3.3 grams; cholesterol, 67 milligrams; sodium, 77 milligrams.

■ Serve this low-calorie, cooked version of the classic Mexican appetizer as the main course for a summer pool party.

Lobster and Crab Ceviche

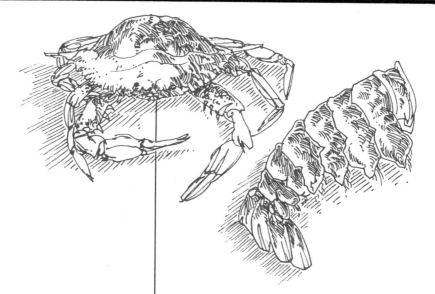

2 fresh or frozen Florida rock lobster tails

1 (16-ounce) can fresh blue crab

2 cups orange juice, freshly squeezed

1 cup lime juice

⅓ cup gold tequila

¾ cup olive oil

1 (4-ounce) can chopped jalapenos, juice included

1 cup cilantro, finely chopped

2 green or red bell peppers, finely chopped

2 tomatoes, chopped

¼ green onions, minced

¼ cup ketchup

¼ teaspoon salt

Freshly ground black pepper

Bring 2 quarts of salted water to a boil and simmer the lobster tails for 8 minutes. Drain and allow to cool. Crack and remove meat. Slice into bite-size chunks. (If using cooked frozen lobster tails, thaw, drain and proceed with recipe.)

Pick over the crab meat and remove any shell or cartilage. Mix together all remaining ingredients. Allow mixture to marinate at least 3 hours before serving.

Makes 14 (½-cup) servings.

Test kitchen notes: This recipe can be prepared up to 2 days in advance. It is traditionally soupy and a little sour. Serve chilled in cups with soda crackers.

Nutrition information per serving: calories, 204; fat, 12.5 grams; carbohydrate, 9.1 grams; cholesterol, 43 milligrams; sodium, 359 milligrams.

■ Crawfish look like miniature lobsters but are milder and sweeter tasting. If you can't find them in their soft-shell state, substitute soft-shell crab.

Soft-Shell Crawfish Stir Fry

2 tablespoons peanut or canola oil
1 medium onion, sliced lengthwise into strips
1 large sweet yellow or red pepper, sliced lengthwise into strips
12 medium soft-shell crawfish
12 fresh large mushrooms, sliced
1 clove garlic, crushed
1 tablespoon low-sodium soy sauce
2 tablespoons mirin wine or sherry

In a large skillet or a wok, heat the oil. When oil is very hot, add onion and cook, stirring constantly, for 3 minutes. Add yellow or red pepper to pan. Cook for 2 minutes longer. Add soft-shell crawfish and mushrooms to the pan and cook, stirring gently for 2 minutes. Soft-shell crawfish should turn bright red as they cook. Be careful not to tear crawfish apart while stirring.

Add garlic, soy sauce and mirin or sherry to the wok. Bring to a boil. Boil for 1 minute, until garlic is fragrant. Remove from heat. Serve hot, with Sesame Rice (page 153) if desired.

Makes 4 servings.

Nutrition information per serving: calories, 225; fat, 8.6 grams; carbohydrate, 7.6 grams; cholesterol, 189 milligrams; sodium, 241 milligrams.

Soft-shell crawfish are growing crawfish that have lost their hard shells and are forming new ones. During this brief period, they are completely edible except for two small calcium deposits behind the eyes. Florida is the nation's largest producer of these soft-shell delicacies, which may some day be as popular as soft-shell crabs.

■ The Geechees are a group of people who live in small communities along the coast of North Carolina, Georgia and North Florida. Their simple cooking is characterized by rice, peppers and seafood.

Geechee Oysters and Rice

1 pint shucked oysters
1 slice thick-cut bacon
1 medium onion
2 cloves garlic
1 green pepper, diced
½ teaspoon salt
½ teaspoon black pepper
1 cup long-grain rice
1½ cups water

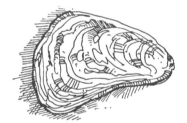

Drain oysters and reserve juice.

Chop oysters into thumbnail-sized chunks; set aside. Dice bacon and fry it in a heavy, covered skillet over medium heat.

As bacon cooks, dice onion, garlic and green pepper. When bacon is brown, add onion to pan and cook until it is soft and translucent. Add garlic and green pepper and cook for 2 minutes longer. Stir in salt, pepper and rice. Make sure rice is well-coated. Add reserved oyster juice and water.

Cover and simmer 10 minutes. Add the chopped oysters, stirring them into the rice. Reduce heat to low and cook 10 minutes longer, until rice is done. Serve immediately with hot sauce, if desired.

Makes 4 servings.

Test kitchen notes: This mild, inexpensive skillet dinner uses a lot of rice and a few oysters. If a meatier dish is desired, stir in chunks of turkey ham, shrimp, fish fillets or boneless chicken. If a spicier dish is desired, add ½ teaspoon cayenne pepper or hot pepper sauce with the salt, pepper and rice.

Nutrition information per serving: Calories, 345; fat, 10.3 grams; carbohydrate, 46.4 grams; cholesterol, 69 milligrams; sodium, 690 milligrams.

■ Rock shrimp earn their name from their hard shells. The meat tastes like lobster but is usually less expensive than other shrimp.

Rock Shrimp Rockefeller

48 rock shrimp in the shell, split, butterflied and cleaned

1 (10-ounce) package frozen spinach, drained

1 tablespoon olive oil

¼ cup shallots, diced

½ cup white wine

¼ cup reduced-calorie, low-cholesterol mayonnaise

¼ teaspoon nutmeg

¼ teaspoon salt

¼ teaspoon freshly ground black pepper

Pinch cayenne pepper

2 tablespoons Pernod or other anise-flavored liqueur

Arrange shrimp on a baking sheet with meat side up. Squeeze excess moisture from spinach. In a skillet over medium heat, fry the shallots in the olive oil until transparent. Stir in the spinach and wine and bring to a rapid boil. Add low-cholesterol mayonnaise, nutmeg, salt, pepper and cayenne pepper. Simmer 2 minutes and remove from heat. Stir in Pernod or anise-flavored liqueur.

Spoon about 1 tablespoon of spinach mixture over each split shrimp. Broil under oven about 4 inches from heat for about 4 to 6 minutes or until tails curl and stiffen.

Makes 6 servings.

Nutrition information per serving: calories, 224; fat, 8 grams; carbohydrate, 6.4 grams; cholesterol, 218 milligrams; sodium, 429 milligrams.

■ Natives of Key West proudly call themselves "conchs" after these sweet, delicious sea snails. Conchs are now a protected species in Florida and Caribbean waters.

Conch Burgers

1 pound cleaned conch, thawed if frozen

½ cup celery, diced

½ cup green onion, finely diced

2 cups whole-wheat bread crumbs

2 egg whites

2 tablespoons reduced-calorie, low-cholesterol mayonnaise

1 tablespoon good-quality mustard

¼ teaspoon cayenne pepper

1 tablespoon ketchup

1 teaspoon fresh lime juice

½ teaspoon salt

¼ teaspoon freshly ground black pepper

½ cup all-purpose flour

¼ cup peanut or canola oil

In a meat grinder or food processor, grind the conch until it is the consistency of chopped clams. Combine in a bowl with celery, green onion, bread crumbs, egg whites, mayonnaise, mustard, cayenne, ketchup, lime juice and salt and pepper. Mix until ingredients stick together. Shape into medium-sized, thin patties. Place on a baking sheet and refrigerate for 30 minutes.

Spread flour on a plate. Gently dredge both sides of each patty in flour. Heat the oil, 1 tablespoon at a time, in a large, heavy skillet. Fry the patties without crowding until golden brown and firm to the touch.

If desired, serve on whole-wheat kaiser rolls with lettuce and tomato.

Makes 6 servings.

Test kitchen notes: Imported conch is usually available frozen in fish markets and well-stocked grocery stores. These light and flavorful burgers are a welcome change from beef or turkey.

Nutrition information per serving (values will vary depending on how much flour adheres when dredged and how well patties are drained of cooking oil): calories, 265; fat, 12.5 grams; carbohydrate, 18.7 grams; cholesterol, 37 milligrams; sodium, 432 milligrams.

■ The more flavorful the fish, the more lively this dish will be. Serve it hot or cold.

Fish Marinated in Vinegar and Vegetables

1½ pounds red snapper, grouper or halibut fillets, sliced about ¼-inch thick
2 tablespoons olive oil
½ cup chopped white onion
2 cloves garlic, crushed through a press
½ cup green bell pepper, chopped
¼ cup peeled, diced green chilies, fresh or canned
½ teaspoon black pepper
½ teaspoon salt
½ cup white-wine vinegar
¼ teaspoon paprika
½ teaspoon dried oregano
¼ cup fresh cilantro or parsley, chopped
2 tablespoons fresh lime or lemon juice
Hot sauce
Lime wedges

Arrange fish in a microwave-safe baking dish. Combine oil, onion, garlic, bell pepper, green chilies, black pepper, salt, wine vinegar, paprika and oregano. Pour over fish.

Cook, covered, in a microwave oven for 5 minutes, turning once on high (100 percent) power. Fish is done when it is firm to the touch and opaque.

Sprinkle with cilantro and fresh lime juice. Serve warm or chilled with hot sauce and lime wedges.

Makes 6 servings.

Nutrition information per serving: calories, 174; fat, 5.8 grams; carbohydrate, 3.3 grams; cholesterol, 100 milligrams; sodium, 125 milligrams.

■ Many people are surprised to learn that alligator is really delicious. It has a meaty flavor almost like pork.

Grilled Cajun-Style Gator Tail

4 ounces gator tail meat (per serving)

Lemon wedges

Seasoning mix:

12 tablespoons paprika

6 tablespoons garlic powder

3 tablespoons salt

3 tablespoons white pepper

3 tablespoons oregano, crushed

3 tablespoons black pepper

2½ tablespoons thyme

1 tablespoon cayenne pepper

To make the seasoning mix, combine paprika, garlic powder, salt, white pepper, oregano, black pepper, thyme and cayenne pepper in jar with a tightfitting lid. Shake well to combine. Mixture may be stored for up to 3 months.

When ready to cook, cut gator tail meat into ½-inch cubes. Roll each cube in 1 tablespoon of the mixture. Cook over high heat on an outdoor barbecue grill or under the oven broiler for 4 to 6 minutes, or until gator tail meat is white and firm to the touch. Serve warm with lemon wedges.

Test kitchen notes: The seasoning mixture will coat up to 24 4-ounce servings of gator tail.

Nutrition information per serving: calories, 283; fat, 5.2 grams; carbohydrate, 4.1 grams; cholesterol, 0 milligrams; sodium, 881 milligrams.

■ Low in fat and rich in flavor, this seafood lasagna is a fine party dish.

Crab and Artichoke Lasagna

Non-stick cooking spray
3 sheets fresh lasagna pasta
 (preferably spinach)
1 pound fresh crabmeat, picked
 over to remove cartilage and
 shell
1 (14-ounce) can artichoke
 hearts (not marinated)
2 tablespoons olive oil
1 shallot, diced
3 tablespoons all-purpose flour
½ teaspoon salt
¼ teaspoon white pepper
1 (8-ounce) clam juice
½ cup skim milk
⅛ teaspoon nutmeg
2 tablespoons white wine
2 cloves garlic
1 cup fresh parsley or basil
16 ounces low-fat ricotta cheese
¼ cup Parmesan cheese
1 egg white
½ cup part-skim mozzarella
 cheese

Preheat oven to 350 F.

Spray a glass baking dish with non-stick cooking spray; set aside. Pick over crabmeat to remove any pieces of cartilage or shells. Cut artichokes into quarters; set aside.

In a saucepan, heat olive oil. Stir in diced shallot and cook for 2 minutes. Whisk in flour, salt and pepper. Cook for 2 minutes over medium heat, until flour sticks to bottom and sides of saucepan. Add clam juice and milk at once. Stir constantly and bring to a boil. Mixture will thicken. Simmer for 2 to 3 minutes. Remove from heat and set aside. Stir in nutmeg, wine and crabmeat.

In the bowl of a food processor or blender, mince garlic and parsley or basil. Add ricotta, Parmesan cheese and egg white. Puree until fine; set aside.

Bring 2 quarts of water to a boil. Trim pasta dough to size of baking dish. Drop trimmed pasta dough into boiling water for 2 minutes. Remove and drain briefly. Continue with each sheet.

Lay 1 sheet of fresh pasta dough in the bottom of the baking dish. Spoon ⅓ of the crab mixture over. Lay half the artichokes on top and cover with ⅓ of the garlic and ricotta mixture. Cover with another sheet of pasta dough. Spread ⅓ of crab mixture on top, and cover with remaining artichokes. Spread with ⅓ of the ricotta mixture. Lay last sheet of pasta dough in pan. Top with remaining crab and ricotta mixtures.

Sprinkle with mozzarella cheese. Bake for 40 minutes. If necessary, place under oven broiler for another 10 minutes to brown surface.

Allow to stand 10 to 15 minutes before serving.

Makes 10 servings.

Test kitchen notes: This is a very rich dish, so small portions go a long way. It is best if made with fresh pasta, which is available in some Italian delicatessens and many large grocery stores. If necessary, substitute dry pasta and cook for 9 minutes according to package instructions.

If desired, substitute shrimp, cooked tuna or mussels in place of the crabmeat. Peas or blanched asparagus can substitute for the artichokes.

Serve with a salad of sliced tomatoes sprinkled with lemon juice.

Nutrition information per serving: calories, 254; fat, 9.8 grams; carbohydrate, 20.1 grams; cholesterol, 62 milligrams; sodium, 463 milligrams.

■ Mild, delicate sole wrapped around a rich-tasting salmon filling looks hard to make, but looks can be deceiving. This elegant dish is surprisingly easy.

Turban of Sole With Salmon Mousse

Non-stick cooking spray

4 fillets of sole or orange roughy, about 1 pound total

¼ teaspoon salt

¼ teaspoon white pepper

½ pound salmon, skinned and boned

2 tablespoons heavy cream

2 egg whites

¼ teaspoon dried dill or tarragon

⅛ teaspoon nutmeg

2 tablespoons dry white wine or vermouth

2 bunches fresh spinach, washed but not drained

1 tablespoon balsamic vinegar or white-wine vinegar

⅛ teaspoon salt

2 tablespoons fresh parsley or dill, minced

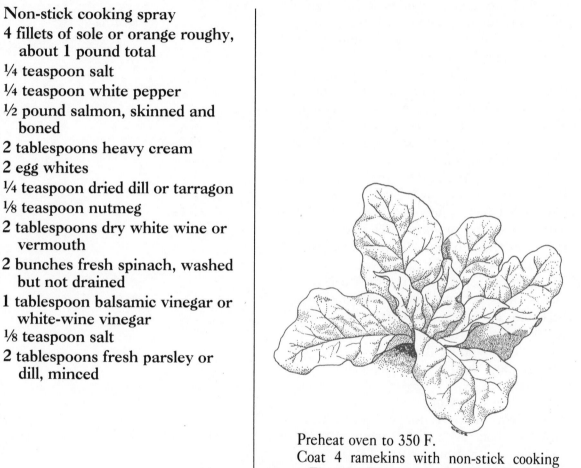

Preheat oven to 350 F.

Coat 4 ramekins with non-stick cooking spray. Fit sole fillets into ramekins, leaving 1 inch of overlap at rim. Trim the excess and use pieces to fill in bottom and up sides of each dish.

Sprinkle fillets with half the salt and pepper. Refrigerate until mousse is prepared.

Combine salmon, remaining salt and pepper, cream, egg whites, dill or tarragon, nutmeg and wine in the bowl of a food processor or blender. Puree until smooth and fluffy. Spoon ¼ cup of mousse inside each sole-lined ramekin. Tap gently to release any air bubbles. Use all mousse. Fold overlapping sole to cover mousse.

Place ramekins in a larger baking pan. Place pan in hot oven and pour enough water in larger baking pan to cover 1 inch of ramekins. Bake for 20 to 25 minutes. Allow to rest 5 minutes before pouring off any accumulated liquid.

Tear spinach into bite-size pieces. Place into a microwave-safe dish or a saucepan. Cook in microwave oven until just wilted, about 2 minutes. Or cook on the stove until wilted, about 4 minutes. Pat dry with a paper towel if necessary.

Spread spinach on individual dinner plates or a serving platter. Sprinkle with balsamic or white wine vinegar and ⅛ teaspoon salt. Run a knife blade around edge of ramekins. Unmold turbans onto spinach bed. Sprinkle with parsley or dill. Serve warm.

Makes 4 servings.

Test kitchen notes: This attractive dish is good as a light main course or appetizer for a dinner party. Or, make in a ring mold for a buffet centerpiece.

Nutrition information per serving: calories, 243; fat, 7.8 grams; carbohydrate, 5.2 grams; cholesterol, 79 milligrams; sodium, 376 milligrams.

■ Sweet papaya, spicy jalapeno pepper and ripe, mellow tomatoes combine to make an easy, truly Floridian dish. Adjust the heat of the salsa according to your tastes.

Broiled Red Snapper With Fresh Papaya Salsa

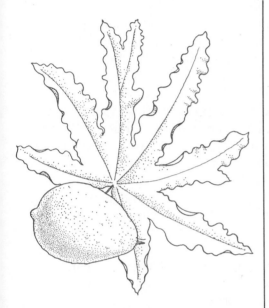

2 teaspoons olive oil

1 small onion, minced

1 small jalapeno pepper, seeded and finely diced

2 cloves garlic, minced or pressed through a sieve

2 tablespoons lime juice

¼ teaspoon ground cumin

¼ teaspoon salt

1 cup ripe fresh papaya, peeled, seeded and diced

1 small tomato, seeded and diced

2 tablespoons cilantro, minced

4 (4- to 6-ounce) red snapper fillets

In a small saucepan, heat 1 teaspoon of the olive oil and cook onion until soft, about 5 minutes. Add jalapeno pepper and cook 3 minutes longer. Reduce heat to low and stir in garlic, lime juice, cumin, salt, papaya, tomato and cilantro.

Bring to a simmer and cook for 5 minutes. Remove from heat and allow to cool while cooking fish.

Preheat oven broiler or outdoor barbecue grill. Brush snapper fillets with remaining olive oil. Broil about 5 inches from the oven element or over medium-hot coals on the outdoor grill. Cook for about 5 minutes, then turn and cook for 5 minutes longer. Fish should be firm to the touch, but not dry.

Divide salsa into 4 portions and spoon a small amount over fish. Pass remaining salsa separately.

Serve immediately with grilled potatoes and steamed zucchini.

Test kitchen notes: Wear rubber gloves when handling jalapeno peppers. The spiciness of salsa can be adjusted to suit personal tastes by using more or less of the jalapeno. For a different flavor, try using fresh or canned pineapple or fresh mango in place of papaya.

Any firm-fleshed fish can substitute for snapper, such as monkfish, mahi-mahi (dolphin), shark, halibut or swordfish.

Nutrition information per serving: calories, 186; fat, 5.1 grams; carbohydrate, 8.7 grams; cholesterol, 43 milligrams; sodium, 36 milligrams.

■ Parchment paper is available in many gourmet food stores and in some commercial bakeries.

Salmon and Herbs Papillote

4 teaspoons olive oil

4 salmon fillets, boneless and skinless

4 sprigs parsley

4 sprigs fresh mint or dill

1 teaspoon dried tarragon

Salt and white pepper to taste

4 sheets of parchment paper or aluminum foil

Preheat oven to 425 F.

Start with 4 (12-by-12-inch) pieces of parchment paper or aluminum foil. Fold the squares in half. Using scissors, cut the squares into heart shapes. Spread open on a work surface.

Rub ½ teaspoon of oil on the bottom of each heart. Top with a salmon fillet and sprinkle parsley, mint or dill, tarragon, salt and pepper over each. Drizzle remaining oil over each fillet.

Fold paper over food. Beginning at the round end of the heart, fold the edges of the heart along the perimeter by pleating it at ¼-inch intervals. Secure the fold by tucking the point underneath. Check to make sure the package is sealed all around. Repeat with remaining hearts.

Place packages on a baking sheet. Bake for 10 minutes. Packages should be puffed. Serve in paper immediately, allowing each person to puncture their own package. Serve

with rice pilaf and a green vegetable.

Makes 4 servings.

Test kitchen notes: Cooking in parchment locks in the fish's natural juices and makes serving and clean-up a snap. The paper or aluminum foil hearts can be readied up to 3 hours before cooking. If desired, bake vegetables such as asparagus, carrots or zucchini in the packets with the fish. Thin slices of lemon, capers, sliced olives or green onions can also be baked in the packets to vary the flavor. Any firm-fleshed fish, such as halibut, sole, flounder or orange roughy can be baked in parchment.

Nutrition information per serving: calories, 346; fat, 20.1 grams; carbohydrate, 0 grams; cholesterol, 123 milligrams; sodium, 94 milligrams.

MEAT

■Americans tend to think of Mexican food as fattening and unhealthy. But this delicious combination of marinated, grilled beef, piquant salsa and mild guacamole is light and nutritious.

Slimline Beef Fajitas

1 pound beef skirt steak or flank steak

¼ cup lime juice

2 tablespoons apple-cider vinegar

3 tablespoons brown sugar

2 cloves garlic, minced

¼ teaspoon salt

1 cup shredded lettuce

1 tablespoon Worcestershire sauce

1 Spanish onion, sliced into strips

1 red bell pepper, sliced into strips

1 cup Skinny Guacamole (page 133)

4 large flour tortillas

½ cup bottled salsa

Trim meat of visible fat. Place in a glass dish. Combine lime juice, apple-cider vinegar, brown sugar, garlic, salt and Worcestershire sauce; pour over beef. Allow to marinate overnight.

Preheat a gas or charcoal-fired grill. When coals are medium-hot, grill meat for 6 minutes per side, basting periodically with marinade. Reserve any extra marinade. Allow meat to rest 10 minutes before slicing into thin strips against the grain. Pour remaining marinade in a heavy skillet. Bring to a boil and simmer the onions until limp and transparent. Add red pepper strips and cook 5 minutes, until marinade begins to boil away and becomes sticky. Remove from heat; keep warm.

Wrap tortillas in foil and heat through. When ready to serve, arrange meat, onions and peppers, salsa, Skinny Guacamole and

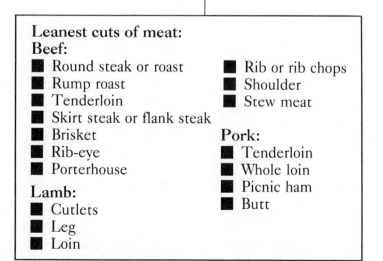

Leanest cuts of meat:
Beef:
■ Round steak or roast
■ Rump roast
■ Tenderloin
■ Skirt steak or flank steak
■ Brisket
■ Rib-eye
■ Porterhouse

Lamb:
■ Cutlets
■ Leg
■ Loin

■ Rib or rib chops
■ Shoulder
■ Stew meat

Pork:
■ Tenderloin
■ Whole loin
■ Picnic ham
■ Butt

lettuce in separate bowls. Each person can take a tortilla and wrap their own fajita with desired fillings.

Makes 4 servings.

Test kitchen notes: In Spanish, fajita means little sash, referring to the thin slices of meat. Skirt steak and flank steak are very lean cuts of beef available in any supermarket or butcher shop. The meat must be sliced very thin or it will be tough. Chicken or turkey breast can be substituted.

Nutrition information per serving: calories, 426; fat, 19.3 grams; carbohydrate, 32.5 grams; cholesterol, 79 milligrams; sodium, 281 milligrams.

■ Inspired by a Japanese dish, this entree retains its Oriental respect for beauty, texture and portion size.

Grilled Beef Rolls in Japanese-Style Sauce

4 spears of fresh asparagus,
   about 5 inches long
8 carrots, cut into 16 strips about
   5 inches long
¾ to 1 pound of boneless
   standing rib roast or top round,
   cut into 4 to 6 thin slices about
   1 inch thick
1 tablespoon cornstarch
1 tablespoon sugar
2 tablespoons water
3 tablespoons mirin
¼ cup low-sodium soy sauce
All-cotton butcher's twine

Blanch asparagus in a microwave oven on high power (100 percent) for 2 minutes until crisp tender. Rinse with cold water and drain; set aside.

Cook carrot strips in a microwave oven on high for 3 to 4 minutes, or until crisp-tender. Rinse with cold water and drain; set aside.

Arrange slices of beef on a work surface. Trim away any visible fat. Using a wooden mallet or heavy ceramic coffee mug, pound meat lightly to a uniform thickness.

Pat meat lightly with cornstarch. Lay 1 asparagus spear lengthwise on each slice of beef. Flank with 2 carrot strips. Roll up tightly and tie securely with butcher's twine.

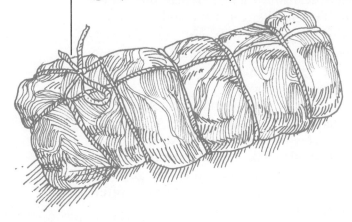

Step 1: Wrap the string once around the meat lengthwise and tie at one end. Without cutting the string wind it around the roll three or four times until you reach the other end. Bring the string back across the roll of meat and tie again at the first knot.

Transfer each roll to a shallow glass dish.

Mix sugar, water, mirin and soy sauce and pour over rolls of beef. Allow to marinate 30 minutes to 1 hour, turning frequently. Heat an outdoor gas or charcoal-fired barbecue grill. Cook over medium-high heat for 5 to 6 minutes, turning twice. Baste twice with marinade. Allow rolls to stand for 5 minutes before removing twine. Slice each roll into 8 pieces and arrange in a fan pattern to show off vegetable stuffing.

Pour remaining marinade in a microwave-safe dish. Heat on full power until simmering. Pour sauce around (not on) beef rolls. Serve immediately.

Makes 4 servings.

Test kitchen notes: If asparagus is out of season, substitute strips of red or yellow pepper cut into 5-inch lengths. Ask the butcher for standing rib roast or prime rib. It is usually available though it may not be on display. The butcher can bone and slice it.

Serve these beef rolls with steamed redskin potatoes or brown rice pilaf and a green vegetable such as zucchini or snow peas to make a complete meal.

Mirin is a low-alcohol, sweet, golden wine made from glutinous rice. A staple of Japanese cooking, mirin adds sweetness to the foods being cooked. It is available at Oriental markets and in the ethnic or gourmet sections of large grocery stores. Mirin is often referred to simply as rice wine.

Nutrition information per serving without mirin: calories, 240; fat, 5.2 grams; carbohydrate, 20.1 grams; cholesterol, 61 milligrams; sodium, 499 milligrams.

■ Olive oil, herbs and lemon juice are the traditional trinity of Greek cooking. In this spring and summer favorite, delicate lamb also plays a starring role.

Grilled Lamb Kebabs With Yogurt-Cucumber Sauce

3 tablespoons olive oil

¼ cup dry red or white wine

1 teaspoon fresh lemon juice

2 bay leaves, crumbled

2 tablespoons fresh oregano or thyme, chopped, or teaspoon dried, crumbled

¼ teaspoon freshly grated black pepper

2 (2-inch) strips lemon zest, minced

2 (2-inch) strips orange zest, minced

1 pound boneless leg of lamb or lamb shoulder, cut into 1-inch cubes

1¼ cups Yogurt-Cucumber Sauce (recipe follows)

Combine the olive oil, wine, lemon juice, bay leaves, oregano or thyme, pepper and lemon and orange zests in a flat glass or ceramic dish. Add the lamb cubes and toss to coat thoroughly. Marinate at least 3 hours or overnight, turning frequently for even distribution of marinade.

Drain meat, reserving marinade for basting. Thread meat on 4 metal skewers. Grill over medium-low coals for 12 to 15 miuntes, turning twice. Baste frequently with marinade. Don't overcook the meat; it should be juicy and pink when served.

Allow meat to stand 10 minutes away from heat. Remove from skewers and serve with new potatoes, red peppers and zucchini that have cooked on the grill alongside the lamb.

Makes 4 servings.

Test kitchen notes: Skewer meat with fruits and vegetables, if desired.

Nutrition information per serving: calories, 338; fat, 21 grams; carbohydrate, 1.2 grams; cholesterol, 104 milligrams; sodium, 88 milligrams.

Yogurt-Cucumber Sauce

1 cup non-fat plain yogurt
1 large clove garlic, crushed
    through a garlic press
3 tablespoons fresh mint,
    chopped, or 1 teaspoon dried
    mint, crumbled
½ teaspoon ground cumin
¼ teaspoon sugar
1 small cucumber, peeled, seeded
    and chopped

Combine all ingredients in the bowl of a food processor or blender. Blend until smooth. Refrigerate at least 3 hours or overnight to allow flavors to blend.

Makes 4 servings.

Nutrition information per serving: calories, 40; fat, 0.2 grams; carbohydrate, 6.3 grams; cholesterol, 1 milligram; sodium, 46 milligrams.

■ The perfect dinner for a rainy evening when you vote to stay indoors and watch a movie. Everyone can cook their own meal in a communal pot of rich, meaty broth.

Chinese Hot Pot Dinner

2 ounces bean thread noodles

¾ pound beef sirloin, sliced wafer-thin

4 green onions, sliced

8 ears miniature corn

½ pound fresh mushrooms, wiped and stems removed

8 ounces fresh spinach, washed and separated

8 ounces fresh napa cabbage, washed and separated

1 pound tofu, drained and cut into cubes

4 quarts hot beef broth

Rice vinegar (for dipping)

Soy sauce (for dipping)

Sesame oil (for dipping)

Soak noodles for 10 minutes in hot water. Drain and cut noodles into 4-inch lengths. Set the dining table so that an electric wok, a Chinese hot pot or an electric frying pan is in the center. Surround the cooking appliance with 4 place settings. On a platter arrange noodles, beef slices, corn, mushrooms, spinach, cabbage and tofu. Bring beef broth to a simmer. Pour into the wok, hot pot or skillet. Adjust appliance heat to simmer. Pass the platter with the food to be cooked. Diners cook the food in the broth using small wire skimmers, fondue forks or chopsticks.

Most food, including meat, cooks in 1 minute or less.

Provide small dishes of rice vinegar, soy sauce and sesame oil for dipping.

Toward the end of the meal, ladle broth into individual soup bowls and serve.

Makes 4 servings.

Test kitchen notes: Large grocery stores carry bean thread noodles, sesame oil and rice vinegar in the ethnic food sections. Oriental grocery stores and some gourmet stores are also good places to shop for these items.

Nutrition information per serving (value for sodium will vary depending on how much rice vinegar and soy sauce adheres to food): calories, 332; fat, 12 grams; cholesterol, 76 milligrams; sodium, 1,701 milligrams.

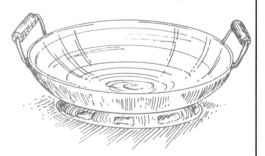

Fast facts

The Chinese hot pot, also called a fire pot, was brought to Peking and Northern China during the Mongolian invasion just before the time of Marco Polo. Entire families would gather around a simmering cauldron, cooking bits of food in the hot broth and dipping them in various sauces. The hot pot dinner was especially popular during the cold winter months.

A traditional Mongolian fire pot looks like a giant bowl with a chimney rising out of the center. A charcoal fire is lit in the chimney and heats the broth in the bowl. However, a fondue pot, electric wok or enamel pot over an electric grill will work just as well. Brass skimmers or fondue forks can be used for removing the food.

The broth ingredients are limited only by the cook's imagination. A variety of vegetables, seafood, shellfish, lean chicken, turkey and noodles lend themselves to this type of cooking. However, avoid high-fat foods such as untrimmed lamb, duck, chicken livers or ham.

Roasted red peppers have just the right touch of natural, smoky sweetness to complement grilled, lean pork.

Pork Loin With Red Pepper Puree

2 red peppers
4 lean, boneless pork loin chops,
  about 3 ounces each
1 tablespoon browning liquid,
  such as Kitchen Bouquet or
  Maggi
4 jumbo mushrooms, wiped
  clean and stems removed

Non-stick cooking spray
Red pepper puree:
3 medium red peppers
1 clove garlic
¼ teaspoon salt
1 teaspoon lemon juice
2 tablespoons cream or sour
  half-and-half

Bell pepper tips

Red and yellow bell peppers are sweeter and have thicker skins than green peppers.

To heighten a pepper's natural sweetness, sprinkle with a pinch of sugar after roasting and peeling.

For a zestier flavor, add a squeeze of fresh lemon juice or sprinkle lightly with balsamic vinegar before serving.

Slice roasted, peeled peppers into long strips and use in salads or sandwiches. The flavorful strips can also be used to top baked potatoes, pasta, toasted bread, grilled chicken or fish.

Puree roasted peppers and freeze to have on hand to add color and flavor to quick sauces for pasta, chicken, fish or meat.

79

Pierce peppers with a knife. Cook over a hot grill until the skins are charred. You can also split peppers in half and char skins under an oven broiler. Put charred peppers into a paper or heavy-duty plastic bag. Let steam and cool inside bag for 10 minutes, or until cool enough to handle. Peel and seed peppers.

Combine pepper flesh with garlic, salt and lemon juice in the bowl of a food processor or blender. Puree mixture.

Add cream in a steady stream while machine is running. If desired, strain sauce through a sieve before serving.

Preheat outdoor grill to medium-high heat or preheat oven broiler. Trim fat from meat. Rub each chop with browning liquid. Grill on one side for 5 minutes. Turn and cook for 7 minutes longer. Remove from heat; keep warm.

Coat a non-stick fry pan with cooking spray. Brown mushrooms, cap side down until golden. Spoon 2 tablespoons of pepper puree over each chop. Top with a mushroom cap.

Serve with wild rice.

Makes 4 servings.

Nutrition information per serving without rice (values are approximate): calories, 235; fat, 11 grams; carbohydrate, 4.2 grams; cholesterol, 83 milligrams; sodium, 217 milligrams.

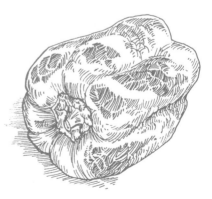

■ This pungent, stir-fried dinner entree is a simple mixture of thinly sliced beef, green onions, carrots and zesty tangerine peel.

Beef With Tangerine Sauce

12 ounces lean beef, such as round steak or flank steak
2 tangerines, sectioned and seeded
2 tablespoons peanut oil
3 tablespoons sherry
2 tablespoons soy sauce
1 tablespoon hoisin sauce
2 cloves garlic, minced
1 teaspoon fresh ginger, minced
2 green onions, cut into ½-inch pieces
2 carrots, cut on the diagonal into ½-inch pieces
Sesame Rice (page 153)

Slice the beef into very thin strips. Refrigerate until ready to use.

Using a vegetable peeler, slice the orange colored outside layer off one of the tangerines. Avoid including too much of the white pith. Slice the colored peel into thin strips. Peel and section the tangerines; set aside. Combine the strips of tangerine peel, sherry, soy sauce, hoisin sauce and garlic; set aside.

Remove beef from refrigerator and arrange all the food near the stove because the actual cooking time is very brief.

Heat the oil in a wok or a large skillet. The oil should be very hot. Add the beef and stir constantly until each piece is cooked. Remove from wok, allowing excess oil to drip back into pan; set beef aside. Add ginger and carrots to the wok. Cook, stirring constantly, for 2 minutes. Add the green onions and continue to cook for 2 minutes longer.

Return the beef to the wok. Add the tangerine sections and hoisin mixture. Bring to a boil, stirring constantly. Boil for 1 minute. Remove from heat and serve immediately.

Makes 4 servings.

Test kitchen notes: Hoisin is available in Oriental markets and in the ethnic foods section of most grocery stores.

Nutrition information per serving: calories, 245; fat, 11.2 grams; carbohydrate, 13.6 grams; cholesterol, 44 milligrams; sodium, 536 milligrams.

■ The delicate licorice flavor of fennel and lean, meaty nuggets of pork give new meaning to the term "skillet dinner." The recipe can be ready in about 30 minutes.

Braised Pork Loin With Fennel

1 pound pork tenderloin, trimmed of all visible fat

2 tablespoons olive oil

2 cloves garlic, crushed through a press

1 small onion, diced

3 tablespoons Pernod or other anise-flavored liqueur

2 bulbs fennel, trimmed and cut into quarters

½ cup white wine

¼ cup water or chicken broth

1 tablespoon tomato paste

¼ teaspoon salt

¼ teaspoon freshly ground black pepper

Cut the tenderloin into 4 serving pieces, about 3 inches long. Heat the olive oil in a large skillet with a tightfitting lid. Brown the pork on all sides. Remove to a separate plate and keep warm. Add the garlic and onion to the skillet and cook until tender and fragrant, about 2 minutes.

Remove skillet from heat and add Pernod or anise-flavored liqueur. Return to heat and bring to a boil, stirring constantly to scrape up brown bits from bottom of the skillet. Return pork tenderloin to skillet and arrange fennel around it. Add white wine, water or chicken broth, tomato paste, salt and pepper. Bring to a boil and reduce heat to a simmer. Cover and allow to simmer gently for 15 to 20 minutes.

Remove pork and fennel from skillet and arrange it on a serving platter or 4 plates. Keep warm. Increase heat under skillet. Boil sauce for 5 minutes until slightly reduced and spoon over pork and fennel.

Makes 4 servings.

Test kitchen notes: If tenderloin isn't available, substitute 4 boneless slices of pork loin, trimmed of visible fat. Brown slices one at a time and proceed with recipe. Turkey breast or skinless chicken will also work well.

Fennel is a bulbous vegetable related to the spice-producing plant called anise. It looks like a fat celery with feathery leaves. Prepare it by trimming away stalks and base. Slice lengthwise into quarters.

Nutrition information per serving: calories, 321; fat, 17.7 grams; carbohydrate, 6.6 grams; cholesterol, 70 milligrams; sodium, 253 milligrams.

■ An outstanding party dish, this sweet-savory stew has its roots in Spanish cooking. It is popular in Puerto Rico, Cuba and Spanish-speaking islands of the Caribbean.

Picadillo al Horno (Baked Spanish-Style Stew)

5 jalapeno peppers
¼ cup olive oil
5 pounds pork (lean shoulder or butt) or 5 pounds lean beef, sliced into fingers with the grain (or a combination half beef and half pork)
4 medium onions, sliced lengthwise into strips
6 cloves garlic, minced
1 (28-ounce) can Italian plum tomatoes, drained and chopped
2 (4-by-1-inch) strips orange peel, without pith
1 cup raisins
1 teaspoon salt
½ teaspoon cinnamon
½ teaspoon ground cloves
½ teaspoon ground allspice
½ teaspoon nutmeg
Freshly ground black pepper
½ cup sherry
3 Granny Smith apples, peeled, cored and sliced into chunks
1 cup pimento-stuffed green olives, halved
½ cup blanched almonds, toasted and coarsely chopped

Peel the peppers by roasting over hot coals or in the flame of a gas stove until the skin is blistered. Place the peppers in a paper sack to steam. When the peppers are cool, put on rubber gloves and peel off skin. Remove stems and seeds and chop; set aside.

Preheat oven to 325 F.

In a Dutch oven or oven-proof casserole, heat oil and fry meat strips in batches until brown. Add the onion and fry until soft. Add the garlic, tomatoes, peppers, orange peel, raisins, spices and sherry. Cook mixture for 10 minutes.

Cover casserole and bake for 1 hour or until meat is tender. Add water only if necessary to prevent the meat from drying out. Recipe can be prepared ahead to this point. Allow mixture to cool and refrigerate, covered.

When ready to complete recipe, preheat oven to 325 F and bake refrigerated mixture for 45 minutes. Skim off any accumulated fat from meat. Using two forks, roughly shred meat into long strips. Stir in the apples and olives and taste for seasoning. Continue baking for 15 minutes. Uncover casserole and bake 15 minutes longer. Just before serving, stir in half the toasted almonds and sprinkle the rest on top.

Makes 14 servings.

Test kitchen notes: Serve this stew hot or at room temperature. Cooked mixture can be used for soft taco fillings. Excellent garnished with Skinny Guacamole (page 133) and salsa.

Nutrition information per serving: calories, 495; fat, 29 grams; carbohydrate, 20.8 grams; cholesterol, 128 milligrams; sodium, 915 milligrams.

Pepper power

■ Chilies are native to the Western Hemisphere though they are now used extensively in Oriental, Caribbean, American and European cooking.

■ Spicy foods actually may cause your metabolic rate to increase. One study found that a group of British volunteers burned off calories an average of 25 percent faster after they ate about a half teaspoon of hot chili sauce.

■ Chili peppers range from thimble-size to more than 8-inch-long pods. As a general rule, the smaller the chili, the hotter the flavor.

■ Chili peppers should be handled with gloves because the chemical that causes hotness, capsaicin, can burn the skin and cause irritation.

■ Most of the heat of the chili pepper is contained in two thin membranes that run down both sides of every pod. For a milder flavor, cut out the membranes and discard the seeds.

■ Pineapple and lamb have a natural affinity for one another. This dish more than proves the point.

Sweet and Sour Lamb

1 (8-ounce) can pineapple pieces, in natural juice
3 tablespoons canola oil
1 large onion, diced
1 cup celery, diced
1 red pepper, seeded and diced
1½ pounds lamb, trimmed of all visible fat and cubed
2 tablespoons finely ground cornmeal
1 teaspoon salt (optional)
2 tablespoons soy sauce
2 tablespoons apple-cider vinegar
¼ teaspoon black pepper
4 cups cooked brown rice

Drain pineapple pieces and reserve juice; set pineapple pieces aside.

Measure juice and add enough water to make 1 cup liquid; set aside.

In a deep skillet heat 2 tablespoons of the canola oil and saute onion for 3 minutes. Stir in celery and red pepper and cook for 3 minutes more. Remove mixture from the skillet.

In the same skillet, heat remaining 1 tablespoon of oil and add lamb. Fry until meat is browned on all sides. Pour off any fat in the skillet; remove pan from heat.

Combine reserved pineapple liquid, finely ground cornmeal, salt, soy sauce, vinegar and black pepper. Return skillet to heat. Pour pineapple liquid mixture into skillet, scraping to remove all brown bits stuck to the bottom of pan. Bring mixture to a boil and add sauteed vegetables and pineapple pieces. Simmer mixture for 50 minutes. Add pineapple pieces and simmer for 10 minutes longer. Serve over cooked brown rice.

Makes 6 servings.

Nutrition information per serving without salt: calories, 474; fat, 16.3 grams; carbohydrate, 43.7 grams; cholesterol, 104 milligrams; sodium, 728 milligrams.

In Jamaica, jerk cooking is the province of "jerk men" who bake the meat slowly in deep earth pits and then char it quickly over the hot coals of a barbecue grill. It is sweet, hot and tender.

Jamaican Jerk Pork

1 pound pork, from the butt or roast, trimmed of all fat

18 whole black peppercorns, ground (about 1 teaspoon)

5 whole allspice berries, ground (about ½ teaspoon)

1 small yellow onion, minced

1 cup green onions, finely chopped

½ teaspoon thyme leaves, ground

½ Scotch bonnet pepper or other hot pepper, minced

3 teaspoons Worcestershire sauce

1 teaspoon sugar

½ teaspoon salt

2 tablespoons vegetable or peanut oil

Slice the pork into slices about 1 inch thick; set aside.

In a blender or food processor, combine the pepper, allspice, onion, green onions, thyme, Scotch bonnet pepper, Worcestershire sauce, sugar and salt. Add the oil by dribbles to make a thick paste.

Smear paste over surfaces of pork.

Marinate meat for at least 3 hours or overnight in the refrigerator. Wrap meat tightly in aluminum foil and bake for 2 hours in a 250 F oven. Remove meat from foil. Over medium-hot coals, grill pork slices for 10 to 15 minutes, basting occasionally with jerk paste and cooking juices.

Makes 4 servings.

Test kitchen notes: The meat becomes very tender in this recipe. The flavor is mild at first, but there is a definite delayed pepper taste.

Nutrition information per serving: calories, 329; fat, 23.4 grams; carbohydrate, 3.7 grams; cholesterol, 97 milligrams; sodium, 403 milligrams.

What is jerk meat?

Jerking is a Jamaican cooking method that involves marinating meat or chicken in a thick paste of allspice, chili, pepper and bay leaf and then baking the meat slowly in a pit and charring it quickly over the hot coals of an outdoor grill before serving.

■ This Vietnamese-style dish is part salad and part pasta, but it is completely delicious. Use the Nuoc Cham as a no-fat dressing.

Barbecued Meat on Rice Vermicelli

1 pound cooked, lean cubed barbecued beef or pork

½ pound rice vermicelli

1 tablespoon sesame oil

1 tablespoon peanut oil

1 cup cucumber, sliced into matchsticks

2 ounces bean sprouts

2 cups green or red leaf lettuce, shredded

¼ cup fresh basil or mint leaves, chopped

¼ cup fresh cilantro, chopped

¼ cup roasted peanuts, coarsely chopped

Nuoc Cham (recipe follows)

Bring 2 quarts of water to a boil. Drop in noodles, cook for 4 minutes and drain. Stir in sesame oil and peanut oil. Divide noodles into 6 bowls and set aside.

Surround each pile of noodles with cucumber, lettuce, mint or basil, cilantro and bean sprouts. Place warm beef or pork on top. Sprinkle with peanuts. Serve with Nuoc Cham on the side.

Makes 6 servings.

Test kitchen notes: Most ingredients listed for this recipe are available at Oriental grocery stores. If you're not familiar with the ingredients, take the recipe with you and the sales staff will help you find what you need. This dish also can be made with cooked shrimp, chicken, turkey or fish. In Vietnamese restaurants, it's frequently served with pieces of crisp spring rolls on top.

Nutrition information per serving (values are approximate): calories, 450; sodium, 52 milligrams; fat, 23.6 grams; carbohydrate, 34.6 grams.

Nuoc Cham

2 cloves garlic, crushed through
   a press
⅛ teaspoon crushed, dried red
   chili pepper
2 tablespoons sugar
2 tablespoons carrot, shredded
2 tablespoons fresh lime juice
   (about ½ lime)
¼ cup rice vinegar
¼ cup fish sauce

In a jar with a tightfitting lid, combine garlic, chili, sugar, lime juice, vinegar and fish sauce.

Shake vigorously until sugar has dissolved. Allow to stand at room temperature until ready to serve. Before serving, garnish with thin shreds of carrot.

Makes 1 cup or 8 servings.

Test kitchen notes: The recipe makes an all-purpose condiment that is indispensable in Vietnamese cooking. It contains the vital tastes — hot, sweet, salty and sour. Rice vinegar is available in Oriental markets and many grocery stores.

Nutrition information per serving: calories, 19; fat, 0 grams; carbohydrate, 4.7 grams; cholesterol, 0 milligrams; sodium, 415 milligrams.

■ Below the Mason-Dixon line, Hoppin' John is a staple for New Year's Day. One taste of this reduced-fat version and you'll understand why Southerners believe eating it brings good luck.

Slim Hoppin' John

1 pound frozen black-eyed peas
4 cups water
½ pound turkey ham
1 medium onion, chopped
¼ teaspoon black pepper
1 whole Scotch bonnet pepper or similar hot chili pepper, such as jalapeno
Salt to taste
1 cup raw, long-grained rice

Fast facts

Though food historians are unsure how the name developed, Hoppin' John has been the South's quintessential dish for New Year's Day for generations.

The protein-rich mixture of black-eyed peas cooked with rice supposedly brings good luck to everyone who eats it.

Put the black-eyed peas and the 4 cups of water in a kettle and bring to a boil. Reduce heat to a simmer.

Slice the turkey ham into chunks and add it to the peas.

Add the whole pepper and onions.

Cover the peas and simmer until peas are tender, about 30 minutes.

When peas are tender but still firm, pour off and reserve the remaining water. There should be about 3 cups. Add more water during cooking if necessary.

Stir the rice, salt and pepper into the peas.

Add cooking liquid back to the pot and return to a boil. Simmer 15 to 20 minutes until liquid is absorbed. Remove kettle from heat and allow to rest on kitchen counter for 10 minutes.

Remove the Scotch bonnet pepper.

Makes 6 servings.

Test kitchen notes: Frozen black-eyed peas are available at most grocery stores. If unavailable, use dried peas, but soak them overnight before using in recipe.

Nutrition information per serving: calories, 210; fat, 2.5 grams; carbohydrate, 32.4 grams; cholesterol, 25.3 milligrams; sodium, 837 milligrams.

■ Comfort foods are those that evoke a feeling of nostalgia for childhood. This meatloaf made with ground turkey and beef is so comforting and delicious it doesn't seem possible it could also be low-fat.

Down-Home Meatloaf and Mashed Potatoes

2 egg whites
½ cup skim milk
½ cup oats
¼ cup yellow cornmeal
1 tablespoon Worcestershire sauce
1 onion, finely chopped
1 carrot, scrubbed and grated
1 clove garlic, crushed through a press
¼ teaspoon salt
¼ teaspoon freshly ground black pepper
1 teaspoon thyme
¼ teaspoon allspice
½ pound ground turkey
½ pound extra lean ground beef
Non-stick cooking spray
1 tablespoon tomato paste
2 teaspoons Dijon-style mustard
1 teaspoon Worcestershire sauce
Mashed Potatoes (recipe follows)

Preheat oven to 350 F.

Combine the egg whites, skim milk, oats and cornmeal in a large bowl. Add 1 tablespoon Worcestershire sauce, chopped onion, grated carrot, garlic, salt, pepper, thyme, allspice, turkey and lean ground beef. Use clean hands or a wooden spoon to thoroughly mix all ingredients.

Coat a loaf pan with non-stick cooking spray. Pack meat mixture into dish, making sure to round the mixture slightly up in the center. Cover meat with aluminum foil.

Bake for 30 minutes.

Mix tomato paste, mustard and 1 teaspoon Worcestershire sauce. If mixture is too thick to brush on loaf, thin with 1 teaspoon of water or apple juice. Increase oven temperature to 375 F.

Remove foil from meat. Brush top of meatloaf with tomato glaze. Return to oven and bake for 10 to 12 minutes longer. Remove from heat and allow meatloaf to stand for 10 minutes before slicing.

Makes 6 servings.

Nutrition information per serving: calories, 218; fat, 7.7 grams; carbohydrate, 14.1 grams; cholesterol, 53 milligrams; sodium, 253 milligrams.

Mashed Potatoes

4 large potatoes, peeled
⅓ cup evaporated skim milk, heated
¼ teaspoon salt
¼ teaspoon white pepper
Pinch of nutmeg
1 tablespoon diet margarine or 1 teaspoon imitation butter-flavored granules

Pierce potatoes with a fork. Place in a microwave-safe baking dish and cover. Cook in the microwave on high power (100 percent) for 8 minutes. Allow potatoes to stand for 3 minutes. Cut potatoes into pieces. Place potatoes in bowl of an electric mixer. Beat on low, adding warm evaporated skim milk by drops.

Gradually increase beater speed and add salt, white pepper, nutmeg and diet margarine or butter-flavored granules. Spoon potatoes in mounds around a platter and spread sliced Down-Home Meatloaf down the center.

Makes 6 servings.

Nutrition information per serving: calories, 167; fat, 1.1 grams; carbohydrate, 34.6 grams; cholesterol, 1 milligram; sodium, 145 milligrams.

How to cut back on fat

Trimming calories from fat doesn't mean giving up your favorite foods. Substituting ground turkey for half the ground beef called for in ordinary recipes reduces the percentage of fat from calories by about half. Ground turkey contains about 15 percent fat; ground beef can contain as much as 30 percent fat.

Extending the amount of meat used with whole grains, such as oatmeal or rice, also cuts down on fat. Using 1 egg white in place of a whole egg reduces fat and cholesterol in a recipe considerably.

■ Cracked wheat, called bulgur in the Middle East, gives this excellent meat dish a nutty crunch. It also greatly reduces the amount of saturated fat in the recipe.

Kibbe and Tomato Sauce

1¼ cups fine bulgur (cracked wheat)

1 cup warm water

1 pound ground lamb

2 medium onions, diced or 1 onion and

1 bunch green onions, diced

½ teaspoon salt

⅛ teaspoon pepper

2 tablespoons toasted pine nuts or walnuts

¼ teaspoon salt

⅛ teaspoon cinnamon

3 tablespoons parsley, chopped

Tomato Sauce (recipe follows)

Place bulgur in a large mixing bowl. Pour the water over bulgur and stir to moisten grains. Allow to stand a few minutes to absorb the liquid. If any water pools in the bottom of the bowl, pour it off.

Add ¾ pound of the lamb to the moist bulgur, reserving ¼ pound for filling. Add salt and pepper and half the onions.

Using wet hands or a wooden spoon, knead the bulgur into the lamb.

Preheat oven to 350 F.

Mix the remaining lamb and onions with the pine nuts or walnuts, salt, cinnamon and parsley. Mix well; set aside.

Spray a baking dish with non-stick cooking spray. Press half the bulgur mixture into bottom of the pan. Cover with lamb and nut mixture. Top with remaining bulgur mixture. Score top with a knife into a diamond pattern. If desired, press a pine nut into the center of each diamond for garnish.

Bake 35 minutes or until brown. Remove from heat and let cool for 5 minutes. Serve with Tomato Sauce (recipe follows), a green salad and pita bread.

Makes 6 servings.

Test kitchen notes: Bulgur (steamed, cracked wheat) is available in health-food stores, Middle Eastern markets and many grocery stores. For this recipe, buy the finest grind.

This recipe can also be prepared in individual oval balls and filled with the stuffing. To make individual meatballs called kibbe bil sanieh, wet hands thoroughly and form the bulgur and meat mixture into 6 portions.

Using a wet finger, form a ½-inch cavity in each ball and stuff with nut mixture. Seal and chill for 30 minutes. Bake in 350 F oven for 25 minutes or until brown.

Nutrition information per serving: calories, 265; fat, 7.4 grams; carbohydrate, 29.1 grams; cholesterol, 52 milligrams; sodium, 338 milligrams.

Tomato Sauce

1 tablespoon olive oil
1 onion, chopped
2 cloves garlic, chopped
1 (15-ounce) can tomato sauce
¼ cup red or white wine
1 bay leaf
½ teaspoon dried basil, crushed
1 tablespoon tomato paste
¼ teaspoon salt
¼ teaspoon black pepper

Heat the oil in a saucepan.

Cook the onions and garlic for 5 minutes, until onion and garlic are golden brown. Do not allow to burn. Add the tomatoes, wine, bay leaf, basil, tomato paste, salt and pepper. Simmer mixture for 15 minutes. Remove bay leaf.

Makes 6 servings.

Nutrition information per serving: calories, 58; fat, 2.5 grams; carbohydrate, 7.3 grams; cholesterol, 0 milligrams; sodium, 530 milligrams.

■Many Puerto Rican people live in Central Florida. The influence of their Spanish heritage is evident in this sweet-and-savory rendition of stuffed squash. Look for chayote squash in Latin American markets.

Chayotes Rellenos Con Carne

2 medium chayote squash

2 tablespoons water

4 ounces extra-lean ground beef

2 ounces extra-lean ham or turkey ham, finely diced

1 small onion, chopped

1 clove garlic, crushed through a press

5 pitted prunes, chopped

¼ teaspoon salt

¼ teaspoon oregano

¼ teaspoon freshly ground black pepper

½ teaspoon capers

2 tablespoons raisins

¼ cup tomato sauce

1 teaspoon cider vinegar

4 oat bran crackers, crushed

How to calculate percentage of calories from fat

Multiply the grams of fat listed in each serving by 9. Divide this number by the total number of calories in each serving. The resulting number is the percentage of calories from fat.

Cut chayotes in half lengthwise. Place in a microwave-safe dish with necks pointing inward. Add water to dish and cover. Microwave on high power (100 percent) for 3 minutes. Turn dish and cook on high for 4 minutes longer. Allow chayotes to stand for 5 minutes. If desired, lightly salt cavities.

Remove and discard oval seed. Using a spoon, scoop out most of pulp, leaving at least a ¼-inch shell. Chop pulp coarsely and set aside while preparing stuffing.

In a non-stick skillet, cook the beef until it begins to lose its pinkish color. Stir in ham or turkey and cook a few minutes longer. Remove pan from heat. Tilt skillet and push meat to one side. Pour off fat.

Return skillet to medium-high heat. Add onion and garlic and cook for 4 minutes, stirring occasionally. Add prunes, salt, pepper, oregano, capers, raisins, tomato sauce, vinegar and squash pulp to skillet. Stir well to coat meat and mix ingredients. Cook for about 5 minutes.

Preheat oven to 400 F.

Divide the stuffing into 4 portions and fill the cavity of each chayote. Top with crushed crackers. Place in a baking dish and bake for 12 minutes. Serve hot.

Makes 4 servings.

Test kitchen notes: Serve these savory-sweet stuffed squash with Orange and Black Olive Salad (page 36) and white rice or cornbread.

Nutrition information per serving using extra-lean ham: calories, 162; fat, 5.8 grams; carbohydrate, 16.6 grams; cholesterol, 30 milligrams; sodium, 446 milligrams.

■ The tenderloin is the leanest and most tender cut of pork. In this fresh-tasting version, the meat can either be served warm or chilled. Take it along for a tailgate feast.

Marinated Pork Tenderloin With Cilantro Mayonnaise

1 pound boneless pork tenderloin, trimmed of fat
2 cloves garlic, minced
1 tablespoon olive oil
1 tablespoon apple cider or red-wine vinegar
¼ teaspoon salt
¼ teaspoon black pepper, freshly ground
¼ cup fresh cilantro, finely chopped
Non-stick cooking spray

Cilantro mayonnaise:
1 cup non-fat plain yogurt
½ cup 1-percent low-fat cottage cheese
¼ cup fresh parsley
¼ cup fresh cilantro
1 tablespoon lemon juice
1 tablespoon Dijon-style mustard
¼ teaspoon white pepper
1 teaspoon corn syrup

Combine yogurt, cottage cheese, parsley, ¼ cup cilantro, lemon juice, Dijon-style mustard, white pepper and corn syrup in a food processor or blender.

Process until smooth and creamy. (Makes about 2 cups.) Refrigerate mixture.

Combine the 2 minced cloves of garlic, 1 tablespoon of olive oil, 1 tablespoon of apple-cider or red-wine vinegar, salt, black pepper and ¼ cup chopped cilantro in an oven-proof, non-metallic dish.

Marinate pork tenderloin for at least 2 hours or overnight, turning frequently.

Preheat oven to 425 F.

Drain pork tenderloin and place on a baking sheet that has been coated with non-stick cooking spray.

Roast the meat for 15 minutes, then reduce heat to 350 F. Brush meat liberally with marinade. Continue roasting for 30 minutes longer. Remove from heat and brush again with marinade.

Allow to cool for at least 15 minutes or longer before slicing into ¼-inch medallions. Arrange on a platter, pouring reserved cooking juices over meat. Serve warm or at room temperature with cilantro mayonnaise.

Makes 4 servings.

Nutrition information per serving: calories, 377; fat, 20 grams; carbohydrate, 8.7 grams; cholesterol, 105 milligrams; sodium, 500 milligrams.

POULTRY

■ Re-create the flavors of Northern India with this exquisite chicken shish kebab.

Tandoori-Style Chicken Brochettes

3 chicken breasts, skinned and boned

3 cloves garlic, crushed through a press

½ teaspoon turmeric

½ teaspoon allspice

½ teaspoon cumin

½ teaspoon paprika

¼ teaspoon salt

¼ teaspoon cardamom

¼ teaspoon white pepper

¼ cup low-fat plain yogurt

2 tablespoons lime juice

Cut chicken into ½-inch pieces and place in a shallow glass container. In a separate dish combine garlic, spices, yogurt and lime juice. Stir to combine. Pour marinade over chicken.

Allow chicken to marinate for at least 1 hour or overnight. Chicken should be very tender. Drain and skewer chicken on skewers. Grill over medium-low heat for 4 to 6 minutes or in an oven broiler for 7 to 10 minutes. Baste occasionally with leftover marinade. Do not allow sauce to burn.

Serve hot with rice or couscous pilaf, grilled onions and a green vegetable such as broccoli, zucchini, green beans or brussels sprouts. A cooling salad of thinly sliced cu-

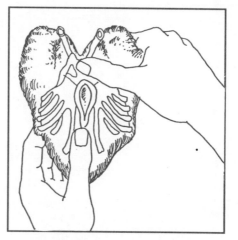

Step 2: To remove keel bone, place a thumb at base of rib cage just above top of keel bone and the other thumb at lower tip of bone. Bend back until bone breaks through membrane. Run finger under edge of keel bone; pull partially away from breast and then pull down to remove white cartillage.

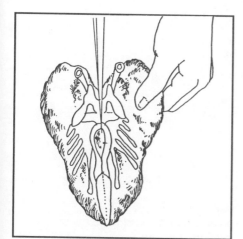

Step 1: Remove skin. Lay breast bone side up. Using a sharp knife, run blade down center to cut thin membrane and expose keel bone (dark spoon-shaped bone) and white cartilage.

cumbers tossed with low-fat yogurt and mint and half a whole-wheat pita bread completes the menu.

Makes 4 servings.

Test kitchen notes: In Northern Indian and Pakistani cooking, a tandoor is a deep, wood-fired clay oven that reaches high temperatures. Food is marinated overnight, skewered and cooked vertically in the hot oven. Spicy-food lovers may want to add a pinch of cayenne pepper.

Nutrition information per serving: calories, 116; fat, 2.3 grams; carbohydrate, 1.8 grams; cholesterol, 55 milligrams; sodium, 205 milligrams.

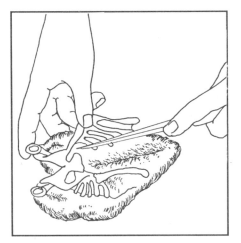

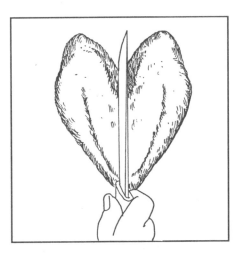

Step 3: To remove rib bones, insert point of knife under long first rib on one side of breast. Resting knife against bones, gently scrape meat away from bones. Cut rib away. Cut through shoulder joint. Remove shoulder joint. Repeat with other side of breast. Locate wishbone at top center of breast; run point of knife close to bone. Remove wishbone.

Step 4: Lay breast flat; cut in half along cleft that contained the keel bone. Remove with tendon. Trim off fat.

■ For picnics, brown-bag lunches or tailgate parties, the flavors of this easy chicken salad are always a hit.

Red, White and Green Chicken Pita

1 cup green seedless grapes
1 cup red seedless grapes
¼ cup chopped pecans
4 ounces low-fat Neufchatel cheese
2 cups cooked chicken, skinned and cut into pieces
3 tablespoons fresh cilantro or parsley, chopped
1 tablespoon whole-grain mustard
2 tablespoons cholesterol-free mayonnaise
1 teaspoon lemon juice
½ teaspoon orange peel
½ teaspoon salt
¼ teaspoon black pepper
Pinch of cinnamon
4 small pita breads, cut in half
8 leaves lettuce

Slice 1 cup of green seedless grapes and 1 cup red seedless grapes in half. Combine sliced grapes, ¼-cup chopped pecans and 4 ounces low-fat Neufchatel cheese in a bowl.

Stir, mashing slightly, until mixture is well-blended. Stir in 2 cups cooked chicken, 3 tablespoons fresh cilantro or parsley, 2 tablespoons cholesterol-free mayonnaise, 1 tablespoon whole-grain mustard, 1 teaspoon lemon juice, orange peel, salt, black pepper and cinnamon.

Line the cut pita breads with lettuce leaves. Stuff filling inside pita bread. Serve immediately with watermelon wedges and cold tea.

Makes 4 servings.

Test kitchen notes: This is an easy recipe to make using leftover turkey, too.

Nutrition information per serving: calories, 348; fat, 13.9 grams; carbohydrate, 26.1 grams; cholesterol, 88 milligrams; sodium, 364 milligrams.

■ Each of these corn bread-stuffed turkey rolls is like a miniature Thanksgiving feast — without the excess fat and calories.

Turkey Scaloppine Rolls With Red Currant Sauce

4 turkey scaloppines, cut from the breast

½ pound ground turkey

¼ teaspoon ground allspice

¼ teaspoon ground thyme

¼ teaspoon ground sage

¼ teaspoon salt

¼ teaspoon black pepper

⅛ teaspoon hot red pepper powder

¾ cup corn bread, crumbled, or corn bread stuffing mix

1 tablespoon olive oil

Red Currant Sauce (recipe follows)

Lay each scaloppine on a work surface. With a bowl or a wooden mallet gently pound meat until each is not more than ¼-inch thick; set aside in refrigerator.

Combine ground turkey, allspice, thyme, sage, salt, black pepper, red pepper and corn bread; mix thoroughly.

Spread about ½ cup of ground turkey sausage on the surface of each scaloppine. Roll up, pinwheel-style. Secure rolls with twine or with toothpicks. Place seam-side down in a baking dish that has been coated with non-stick spray.

Preheat oven to 325 F.

Rub surface of each roll with olive oil, then rub a sheet of baking parchment paper with oil. Cover rolls with parchment and bake for 25 minutes or until done.

Serve turkey rolls hot with Red Currant Sauce, oven-baked sweet potato spears and a green vegetable.

Makes 4 servings.

Test kitchen notes: The rolls may be frozen, either cooked or raw, for up to 4 weeks. For an attractive serving presentation, slice the rolls into medallions. The sauce will freeze for up to 4 weeks.

Nutrition information per serving (values will vary depending on how much sauce adheres to food): calories, 498; fat, 12 grams; carbohydrate, 34 grams; cholesterol, 28 milligrams; sodium, 851 milligrams.

Red Currant Sauce

1 teaspoon peanut oil
1 shallot, minced or ½ small yellow onion, minced
1 clove garlic, minced
½ cup chicken broth
3 tablespoons raspberry or red-wine vinegar
1 tablespoon lemon juice
1 tablespoon port or Marsala wine
2 tablespoons red currant jelly
1 teaspoon cornstarch, mixed into a paste with 1 teaspoon port or Marsala or water

While turkey is cooking, heat oil in a saucepan and saute onion until transparent and pale golden. Add garlic and cook 1 minute longer. Add chicken broth, vinegar, lemon juice, wine and jelly. Bring to a boil. Reduce heat and simmer for 10 minutes. Taste for seasoning. If necessary, adjust sweet-sour ratio by adding more lemon juice or more jelly.

If desired, strain sauce. Before serving, stir cornstarch paste into sauce. Bring sauce to a boil and cook until sauce thickens.

Makes about 1 cup.

Nutrition information per 2-tablespoon serving: calories, 28; fat, 0.8 gram; carbohydrate, 4.7 grams; cholesterol, 0 milligrams; sodium, 64 milligrams.

Fast facts

Good and Bad Cholesterol:

One form of cholesterol, known as HDL (high density lipoprotein or "healthy" lipoprotein) is associated with a decreased risk of heart disease. HDL transports excess cholesterol to the liver, where it can be excreted out of the body.

LDL (low density lipoprotein or "lousy" lipoprotein) transports and deposits cholesterol. If the LDLs transport more cholesterol than the cells can use, the excess forms a plaque, which builds up in the arteries. This buildup causes atherosclerosis, a precursor to heart attacks and strokes.

■ This is the perfect Florida summer entree — the kind to cook outdoors while you admire the sunset. Serve it with a robust, refreshing corn relish.

Grilled Chicken With Corn Relish

2 teaspoons corn oil, divided
1 small yellow onion, minced
1 clove garlic, minced
¼ cup cider vinegar
2 tablespoons lime juice
2 tablespoons honey
¼ teaspoon hot pepper sauce
¼ teaspoon ground cumin
1 cup corn, fresh or frozen
2 tablespoons red pepper, minced
2 tablespoons green pepper, minced
4 chicken breast halves, boned and skinned

In a small saucepan, heat 1 teaspoon corn oil over medium-high heat. Cook onion until lightly brown, about 5 minutes. Add garlic and cook 1 minute longer. Stir in vinegar, lime juice, honey, hot sauce and cumin. Bring to a boil and cook for 5 minutes. Reduce heat to a simmer, add corn and peppers.

Simmer for 3 to 4 minutes; remove from heat. Heat a charcoal or gas grill to medium. Rub chicken breasts with remaining corn oil. Grill chicken for 5 minutes on 1 side, basting often with liquid from corn relish. Turn chicken breasts and grill for 5 more minutes, basting frequently with corn-relish liquid.

Chicken is done when breasts are firm to the touch. Serve immediately with ¼ cup of relish for each breast.

Makes 4 servings.

Test kitchen notes: The relish can be made in advance and frozen for up to 3 months until ready to use. It will keep 1 week in the refrigerator.

Nutrition information per serving: calories, 416; fat, 8.5 grams; carbohydrate, 29.5 grams; cholesterol 146 milligrams; sodium, 134 milligrams.

■ Lean, juicy chicken served with a bold basil pesto sauce and mellowed with spinach fettuccine — this is the kind of meal you can savor year-round.

Chicken With Pesto Sauce and Spinach Fettuccine

4 chicken breasts, boned and skinned

1 tablespoon olive oil

½ teaspoon salt

¼ teaspoon black pepper

Low-Fat Pesto Sauce (recipe 149)

2 tablespoons dry white wine or vermouth

8 ounces spinach fettuccine, cooked, drained, and tossed in cooking liquid reserved from chicken breasts

Wash chicken breasts and pat dry with a paper towel.

Rub with oil and sprinkle with salt, pepper and wine. Place in a microwave-safe baking dish and cover with waxed paper.

Microwave on high (100 percent power) for 4 minutes. (Times may vary according to the wattage of individual microwave ovens.)

Turn breasts over and spoon some of the liquid over each. Cover and cook on high for 3 to 5 minutes more, until chicken is opaque and firm to the touch. Do not overcook or chicken will be tough and dry.

Toss cooked fettuccine in leftover cooking liquid. Arrange chicken on 4 plates.

Spoon 2 tablespoons of Low-Fat Pesto Sauce (recipe 149) over each breast. Divide fettuccine into 4 portions and, if desired, spoon additional pesto over pasta.

Makes 4 servings.

Nutrition information per serving including pesto: calories, 514; fat, 17.6 grams; carbohydrate, 25.6 grams; cholesterol, 148 milligrams; sodium, 653 milligrams.

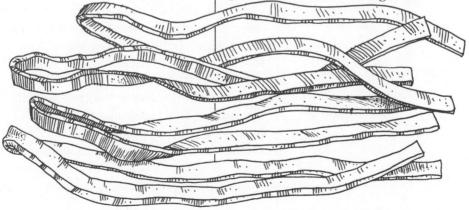

■ Delicious and low in fat, this white-meat version of cannelloni balances a delicately spiced filling with a zesty Marinara Sauce.

Chicken Cannelloni

8 cannelloni pasta shells, dried
1 cup fresh white bread crumbs
½ cup skimmed milk
¾ pound boneless chicken breasts, skinned (about 3)
1 shallot or mild, white onion
2 egg whites
2 tablespoons whipping cream
½ teaspoon salt
¼ teaspoon white pepper
¼ teaspoon allspice
¼ teaspoon thyme
Non-stick cooking spray
1½ cups Marinara Sauce (recipe 122)
¼ cup water
¼ cup Parmesan cheese, grated

Bring a kettle of lightly salted water to a rolling boil. Add the cannelloni shells. Cook according to package directions until tender, about 7 to 9 minutes. Do not overcook. Drain in a colander until almost dry; set aside.

In a microwave-safe bowl, combine crumbs and milk. Cook on high (100 percent) power for 1 minute. Stir and cook on high for 1 minute longer; set aside to cool.

In the bowl of a food processor or meat grinder, combine chicken and shallot. Puree until creamy looking. Add the milk and breadcrumb mixture, egg whites, cream, salt, white pepper, allspice and thyme. Puree until mixture is fine and no lumps remain. Preheat oven to 375 F. Coat a baking dish with non-stick cooking spray.

Spoon chicken mixture into cannelloni. Place the stuffed cannelloni in the baking dish. Pour Marinara Sauce and water over the top. Cover and bake for 30 to 35 minutes, until sauce is bubbly and chicken mixture is firm. Sprinkle with Parmesan cheese. Let stand 5 minutes before serving.

Makes 8 servings.

Test kitchen notes: Different brands of pasta vary greatly in sodium and nutritional content, so before buying cannelloni shells, read and compare labels. Look for the brand that is lowest in sodium, fat and calories.

Nutrition information per serving without sauce (values will vary depending on brand of pasta): calories, 269; fat, 5.2 grams; carbohydrate, 25.3 grams; sodium, 295 milligrams.

■ This tangy, filling salad would be as appropriate at a luncheon or a Super Bowl party. Hazelnut oil gives it a special nutty flavor but another oil would work as well.

Smoked Turkey, Apple and Hazelnut Salad

1 pound smoked turkey breast, skinned and cubed

3 tart green apples, such as Granny Smith, cored and diced

2 cups celery, diced

¼ cup hazelnuts (filberts), toasted

12 ounces fresh spinach, torn into bite-size pieces

Lemon and Hazelnut Dressing (recipe 152)

12 leaves romaine lettuce

1 tablespoon hazelnut oil

6 lemon wedges

Toss the turkey chunks, green apples, celery and half the hazelnuts together. Pour half the Lemon and Hazelnut Dressing over and toss again. Cover and refrigerate until ready to serve.

Line eight plates with romaine leaves. Make a bed of the spinach on top of lettuce and mound the turkey salad on top. Garnish with remaining hazelnuts and lemon wedges. Drizzle with Lemon and Hazelnut Dressing. Drizzle ¼ tablespoon of hazelnut oil over each serving at the last minute.

Makes 8 main-course servings.

Nutrition information per serving: calories, 167; fat, 7.6 grams; carbohydrate, 11 grams; cholesterol, 32 milligrams; sodium, 451 milligrams.

Children can suffer from high cholesterol

■ A diet high in saturated fat and cholesterol is the main cause of high blood cholesterol in children.

■ Children as young as 5 can begin to develop high blood cholesterol.

■ High blood cholesterol isn't something that a child will outgrow. It stays high and tends to increase with age, unless something is done about it.

■ According to the American Heart Association, less than 30 percent of a child's total daily calories should come from fat.

■ Inspired by a recipe of my mother's, this fast and easy Southwestern dinner features spicy chicken on a bed of garlicky zucchini. For the most authentic flavor, look for mild New Mexican red chili powder.

Rio Grande Chicken

4 chicken thighs, skinned

¼ teaspoon salt

½ teaspoon red chili powder (not cayenne)

¼ teaspoon cumin

¼ teaspoon black pepper

½ teaspoon sugar

3 medium-sized zucchini squash or 4 small zucchini, grated and drained in a colander (about 2½ to 3 cups)

1 teaspoon olive oil or canola oil

2 cloves garlic, crushed through a press

¼ teaspoon salt

1 cup prepared commercial mild or medium-hot salsa

4 teaspoons sour cream or imitation sour cream

With a sharp knife, make a slit in the underside of thighs along each side of the bone. Remove the bones and trim away any cartilage.

Using a coffee mug or meat pounder, pound the boned thighs until they are a uniform thickness. Roll up and secure with a toothpick.

In a shallow dish or on a plate, combine the salt, red chili powder, cumin, black pepper and sugar. Stir to blend. Roll each thigh lightly in the spice mixture to lightly coat the surface.

Preheat a barbecue grill. Cook thighs over medium-high heat until meat is firm to the touch. Be careful not to allow the sugar to burn. (Chicken can also be cooked over medium-low heat in a non-stick skillet.) Meat should cook in about 10 minutes. Remove toothpicks.

Heat oil in a non-stick skillet. Add crushed garlic and grated, drained zucchini. Sprinkle with salt and stir well to mix flavors. Cook stirring frequently for 3 to 4 minutes, until zucchini just crisp-tender and begins to look watery. Divide into 4 portions and place a chicken thigh atop each.

In a microwave-safe dish warm the salsa on high (100 percent) power for 1 minute. Or heat the salsa on the stovetop until warm to the touch. Spoon ¼ cup over each chicken thigh. Top with 1 teaspoon sour cream or imitation sour cream.

Makes 4 servings.

Nutrition information per serving: calories, 156; fat, 7.8 grams; carbohydrate, 7.2 grams; cholesterol, 48 milligrams; sodium, 350 milligrams.

■Turkey paired with tart cherries is a sublime combination. The garnet-colored sauce is easy and fast because it can be made with frozen cherries.

Turkey Breast Montmorency

Tips on how to reduce fat in cooking

Select lean cuts of meat, white meat of chicken or turkey, fish or seafood.

Trim all visible fat off meat.

Broil, bake or steam instead of frying foods.

Use skim-milk and low-fat dairy products in recipes.

Remove skin from chicken and turkey before serving.

Grill, broil or roast meat on a rack to allow fat to drip off.

Use non-stick cooking spray instead of oil, margarine or butter to keep food from sticking to pans.

Cook with non-stick pans.

Non-stick cooking spray

4 slices turkey breast or cutlets, about 4 ounces each

2 tablespoons canola or peanut oil

2 shallots, minced

¼ cup red wine

1 tablespoon brandy

1 tablespoon soy sauce

¼ cup chicken broth

½ cup tart frozen pitted cherries, drained, with juices reserved

2 tablespoons honey

1 tablespoon cornstarch

1 tablespoon apple juice

Coat a non-stick frying pan with non-stick cooking spray. Add the oil and heat over medium-high heat. Saute the turkey slices until the meat turns opaque. Turn and cook on the other side, about 4 minutes. Remove to a warm platter or individual plates and keep warm in a 200 F oven.

Increase the heat under the skillet to medium high. Saute the minced shallots until soft and transparent. Add the red wine to the skillet and using a wooden spoon, scrape up any brown bits. Add the brandy, soy sauce, chicken broth, reserved cherry juice and honey. Bring to a vigorous boil. Cook until liquid is reduced by half. Turn down the heat to a simmer. Add the cherries and heat through.

Mix the cornstarch with the apple juice to form a paste. Stir the mixture into the hot cherry sauce and cook until it thickens. Remove from heat. Spoon 2 tablespoons of the sauce, including the cherries, over the warm turkey fillets. Pass the remaining sauce separately.

Makes 4 servings.

Test kitchen notes: This is a modern adaptation of a French recipe traditionally made with the dark, sweet Montmorency cherries. Sweet cherries can be used in this recipe, but reduce the amount of honey and increase the soy sauce. Serve with brown rice or pureed sweet potatoes and a green vegetable such as brussels sprouts or broccoli.

Nutrition information per serving: calories, 265; fat, 7.6 grams; carbohydrate, 13.5 grams; cholesterol, 82 milligrams; sodium, 303 milligrams.

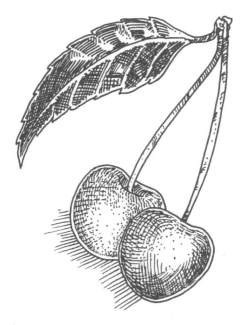

■ These not-too-spicy, low-fat enchiladas have been a consistent winner every time they were served. The salsa keeps them moist.

Chicken Picadillo Enchiladas

1 (16-ounce) can stewed tomatoes

1 cup picante sauce

3 cups shredded or diced cooked chicken

1 red bell pepper, chopped

¼ cup dark raisins

¼ cup coarsely chopped slivered toasted almonds

⅛ teaspoon cinnamon

1 garlic clove, minced

Non-stick cooking spray

12 (7- to 8-inch) flour tortillas

1 cup (4 ounces) shredded Monterey Jack cheese

Ripe olive slices, for garnish

Chopped tomatoes, for garnish

Combine tomatoes, ¾ cup of the picante sauce, chicken, red pepper, raisins, almonds, cinnamon and garlic in 10-inch skillet.

Bring to a boil; reduce heat and simmer uncovered 10 minutes or until most of liquid is absorbed. Spoon ⅓ cup chicken mixture down center of each tortilla. Coat a 13-by-9-by-2-inch dish with non-stick cooking spray. Roll up tortillas and place in dish seam-side down. Spoon remaining ¼ cup picante sauce evenly over tortillas.

Cover with foil.

Bake at 350 F for 20 minutes or until heated through.

Sprinkle with cheese; let stand 5 minutes. Garnish as desired and serve with additional picante sauce.

Makes 12 enchiladas.

Test kitchen notes: Trim calories and fat off this recipe by purchasing tortillas made without lard.

Nutrition information per wrapped tortilla without garnish: calories, 308; fat, 11.6 grams; carbohydrate, 30.4 grams; cholesterol, 57.8 milligrams; sodium, 515 milligrams.

■ This modern interpretation of the classic flat Tex-Mex enchilada combines low-fat turkey with all the trimmings.

Turkey Enchilada Tortas

1 pound ground turkey
1 small onion, chopped
1 clove garlic, minced
1½ cups picante sauce
1 (8-ounce) can tomato sauce
1 teaspoon ground cumin
1 cup chopped green pepper
1 tablespoon ripe olives, drained and sliced
1 (8-ounce) can whole kernel corn, drained, or 1 cup frozen whole kernel corn
12 (7- to 8-inch) flour tortillas
1 cup shredded Cheddar cheese
Shredded lettuce, for garnish
Chopped tomato, for garnish
Chopped avocado, for garnish

Cook turkey with onion and garlic in 10-inch skillet until no longer pink. Drain. Add 1 cup of picante sauce, tomato sauce and cumin; simmer 5 minutes. Add green pepper, corn and olives; simmer 5 minutes or until most of liquid is evaporated. Place 4 flour tortillas on large greased cookie sheet. Reserve ¼ cup of the cheese. Spoon half of turkey mixture evenly over tortillas; sprinkle with small amount of cheese.

Repeat layering, ending with tortillas.

Spoon remaining ½ cup picante sauce evenly over tortillas, spreading to edges. Sprinkle with reserved cheese.

Bake at 350 F for 15 to 20 minutes or until hot.

Garnish as desired and serve with additional picante sauce.

Makes 6 servings.

Test kitchen notes: Shop for tortillas made without lard. Many brands are now made with vegetable shortening.

Nutrition information per serving: calories, 470; fat, 17 grams; carbohydrate, 58.5 grams; cholesterol, 19.8 milligrams; sodium, 972 milligrams.

■You can get the authentic island flavors by using a commercial jerk seasoning mixture. The slow cooking makes the chicken falling-off-the bone tender.

Jamaican Jerk Chicken

4 chicken breasts, skinned but with bone in

2 to 3 teaspoons commercial Jamaican jerk seasoning (or use recipe from Jamaican Jerk Pork, page 86)

Wash breasts thoroughly. Smear chicken with seasoning, coating thinly for medium spice and thickly for a fiery taste.

Place in a buttered glass dish, cover and marinate in the refrigerator for at least 2 hours but no more than 3 hours. Preheat oven to 200 F. Bake in preheated oven for 2 to 2½ hours. Near the end of baking time start coals in an outdoor grill or turn on a gas grill.

Remove chicken from oven and immediately place the breasts on grill. Cook the chicken breasts an additional 10 to 15 minutes or until the outside is crispy.

Makes 4 servings.

Test kitchen notes: Jamaican jerk seasoning is available in several brands in many large grocery stores, gourmet shops and West Indian markets.

Nutrition information per serving using seasoning mix on page 86: calories, 334; fat, 20.3 grams; carbohydrate, 5.6 grams; cholesterol, 93 milligrams; sodium, 423 milligrams.

■ The flavors of pumpkin, sherry and cream make this dish a mellow autumn indulgence. Serve it with a light salad.

Chicken Breasts With Sherry Pumpkin Sauce

4 chicken breast halves, boned and skinned

1 tablespoon peanut or olive oil

¼ cup dry sherry

1 clove garlic, crushed

4 tablespoons whipping cream

¼ cup pumpkin puree, fresh or canned

¼ teaspoon salt

¼ teaspoon white pepper

¼ teaspoon nutmeg

¼ cup toasted pecans

In a large, non-stick skillet, heat the oil. Without crowding, add the chicken breasts and saute over medium high heat.

Cook about 4 to 5 minutes per side, until the breasts are firm to the touch and no pink remains.

Remove to a heated platter and keep warm. Chicken breasts will continue to cook slightly while the sauce is being made.

Add the sherry to the hot skillet.

Bring to a boil, scraping up the browned bits from the bottom and sides. Add the crushed garlic, cream, pumpkin, salt, pepper and nutmeg.

Reduce the heat and allow to simmer 3 minutes or until thickened. Pour over chicken breasts and garnish with toasted pecans.

Makes 4 servings.

Test kitchen notes: This satiny sauce makes a deliciously different entree in about 30 minutes.

Nutrition information per serving: calories, 282; fat, 15.4 grams; carbohydrate, 3.5 grams; cholesterol, 69.2 milligrams; sodium, 230 milligrams.

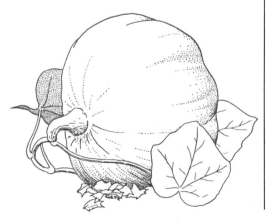

■ The sweetness of the winter squash perfectly balances the chicken and the mild licorice flavor of the tarragon. Freeze the salad and reheat in the microwave for a fast luncheon or supper dish.

Chicken-Stuffed Acorn Squash

2 medium-size acorn squash
3 tablespoons chopped scallion
1 medium apple, cored and diced
2 cups cooked, cubed chicken
1/3 cup chopped walnuts
2 tablespoons freshly squeezed lemon juice
1/2 teaspoon dried tarragon
1/4 teaspoon dried thyme
2 tablespoons cholesterol-free mayonnaise
Lemon wedges

Pierce whole squash through to center in several places with long metal skewers or a sharp knife. Place at opposite corners of microwave oven on paper towel. Microwave on high power (100 percent) for 5 minutes, turn over; microwave 5 minutes more or until soft to the touch. Let stand 5 minutes. Cut in half vertically.

Discard seeds and fibers. Scoop out about 1/3 cup pulp from each half. In a large bowl, combine scallions, apple, chicken, walnuts, lemon and herbs. Stir in reserved squash pulp and mayonnaise, stirring well to coat ingredients.

Spoon filling into squash halves. Place in a non-metal baking dish, cover with waxed paper.

Microwave 8 minutes on medium power (50 percent) or until heated through. Serve with lemon wedges.

Makes 4 servings.

Nutrition information per serving: calories, 415; fat, 17.2 grams; carbohydrate, 31.7 grams; cholesterol, 104 milligrams; sodium, 149 milligrams.

Fast facts

The Human Nutrition Information Service of the U.S. Department of Agriculture recommends the ideal daily diet should include:

■ Three to 6 servings of whole-grain bread, cereal, barley, couscous, oatmeal or cooked pasta or rice.

■ Two to 4 servings of fresh fruit.

■ Three to 5 servings of vegetables, such as green leafy vegetables, yellow vegetables (winter squash) or starchy vegetables (potatoes or fresh beans).

■ Two to 3 servings of lean meat, poultry, fish, cooked beans, nuts or seeds.

■ Two servings of low-fat milk, low-fat cheese or low-fat yogurt.

■ Sesame seeds form a nutty crust on the chicken. The tangy balsamic vinegar keeps the dish from tasting too rich.

Sequined Chicken

4 chicken breast halves, about 3½ to 4 ounces each, skinless and boneless

⅓ cup sesame seeds

2 tablespoons canola oil

¼ teaspoon salt

2 tablespoons balsamic vinegar

¼ teaspoon freshly ground black pepper

3 tablespoons defatted chicken broth

3 tablespoons white wine

2 tablespoons unsalted butter (not margarine)

Using a coffee mug, gently pound thickest part of chicken breasts to be even with the thinnest part. Sprinkle with salt and pepper.

Pour sesame seeds on a plate. Dredge chicken breasts in seeds, patting gently to make them adhere. Heat oil in a large saute pan. Cook the chicken breasts on one side on medium-high heat until they begin to stiffen and look opaque, about 5 minutes.

Turn and cook on other side, regulating heat to keep the seeds from burning. Cook until done, about 4 to 5 minutes.

Remove chicken to warm plates and keep warm. Discard all fat in pan but keep as many seeds as possible. Increase heat to high. Add vinegar, chicken broth and wine to the pan. Bring to a hard boil. Use a wooden spoon or spatula to scrape off any brown bits from side of pan. Boil until liquid reduces by half, about ¼ cup. Stir in butter, 1 tablespoon at a time, until the sauce begins to look glossy. Pour 1 to 1½ tablespoons of sauce over each chicken breast.

Makes 4 servings.

Test kitchen notes: As the sauce cooks down, it becomes tart but not vinegary. Serve with braised brussels sprouts and carrots and half a baked potato per person. Top the potato with mild Mexican salsa instead of butter.

Nutrition information per serving: calories, 333; fat, 22.2 grams; carbohydrate, 2.8 grams; cholesterol, 89 milligrams; sodium, 212 milligrams.

■An orange-flavored sauce combined with sweet onions makes this roasted game hen a fabulous autumn or winter entree. The barley pilaf absorbs the delicious juices.

Honey-Glazed Cornish Hens

2 (1½-pound) Cornish hens
1 teaspoon fresh orange peel, grated
3 tablespoons lemon juice
4 tablespoons orange juice concentrate, thawed
2 tablespoons soy sauce
1 clove garlic, minced
1 tablespoon orange blossom honey
½ teaspoon onion powder
¼ teaspoon thyme
Non-stick cooking spray
1 medium onion, chopped
1 teaspoon cornstarch
½ cup fresh orange sections

Thaw hens overnight in refrigerator.

When ready to cook, preheat oven to 350 F.

Remove giblets from cavity.

Place breast side down on a cutting board and cut in half along backbone.

Remove skin and fat, discard.

If desired, bone breast section of Cornish hen, leaving drumstick and wing bones intact.

In a small microwave-safe dish, combine orange peel, lemon juice, orange juice concentrate, soy sauce, honey, garlic, onion powder and thyme.

Heat to boiling in microwave oven; set aside.

Coat a baking dish with non-stick cooking spray.

Divide chopped onion into 4 portions and place hens bone side down on onions.

Pour orange juice mixture over birds.

Bake for 45 minutes, basting every 10 to 15 minutes with cooking juices.

If birds brown too quickly cover loosely with aluminum foil.

If birds brown too slowly, at end of cooking time, cook for 5 minutes under oven broiler.

When birds are done, remove from baking dish to warm dinner plates keeping chopped onions underneath.
Garnish with orange slices.

Spoon any fat off remaining juice mixture in baking dish.

Mix pan juices with cornstarch and heat just to boiling and sauce thickens. Pass sauce separately.

Makes 4 servings.

Test kitchen notes: Serve with Barley Pilaf (recipe 155) and yellow squash or sauteed red and green pepper and carrots.

Nutrition information per serving (values are approximate): calories, 271; fat, 15 grams; carbohydrate, 21.1 grams; cholesterol, 137 milligrams; sodium, 414 milligrams.

■ Turkey has taken the place of ground beef in many American homes. This burger recipe redefines a classic.

Turkey Burgers With Cranberry Ketchup

¾ pound ground turkey

1 cup fresh whole-wheat bread crumbs (approximately 2 slices)

1½ tablespoons cholesterol-free mayonnaise

1 tablespoon fresh parsley or basil, chopped

½ teaspoon salt

¼ teaspoon thyme

¼ teaspoon nutmeg

4 leaves lettuce

1 medium tomato, cut into 8 slices

4 whole-grain buns

Cranberry Ketchup (recipe follows)

Combine the ground turkey, bread crumbs, mayonnaise, parsley or basil, salt, thyme and nutmeg in a large bowl. Mix well with your hands. Divide into 4 generous patties.

Cook on an outdoor grill over low coals for about 4 minutes per side. Or, lightly coat a non-stick skillet with non-stick cooking spray. Cook burgers, without crowding, about 4 minutes per side.

Serve on whole-grain buns with 2 tomato slices, lettuce and Cranberry Ketchup.

Makes 4 servings.

Nutrition information per serving with ketchup: calories, 355; fat, 10.8 grams; carbohydrate, 47.6 grams; cholesterol, 89.5 milligrams; sodium, 876 milligrams.

Cranberry Ketchup

½ cup cranberry sauce

2 tablespoons tomato paste

1 tablespoon cider vinegar

¼ teaspoon onion powder

¼ teaspoon white pepper

¼ teaspoon salt

Combine cranberry sauce, tomato paste, vinegar, onion powder, pepper and salt in a microwave-safe dish or small saucepan.

Cook over medium-low heat or in the microwave on medium (50 percent) power until cranberry sauce melts, stirring occasionally.

Cool to room temperature. Serve 2 tablespoons cranberry ketchup on the side.

Makes 4 servings.

Nutrition information per serving: calories, 60; fat, 0.1 gram; carbohydrate, 15.2 grams; cholesterol, 0 milligrams; sodium, 162 milligrams.

MEATLESS MEALS

■ This slimmed-down pizza is made in the colors of the Italian flag — red, white and green.

Tomato and Basil Pizza on Whole-Wheat Crust

½ recipe for Whole Wheat Bread
  Sticks (page 168)

2 cups part-skim mozzarella
  cheese, grated

6 roma tomatoes, thinly sliced

2 teaspoons olive oil

¼ teaspoon freshly ground black
  pepper

1 cup fresh basil leaves, shredded,
  or 1 teaspoon dried basil,
  crumbled

Preheat oven to 425 F.

Roll out dough to cover a 12-inch pizza pan or earthenware pizza stone. (Pizza stones, sometimes called baking stones or tiles, are available at cookware stores or through mail-order catalogs. The porous stone surface absorbs moisture from the dough, giving it a crusty texture.)

Cover dough evenly with cheese. Place tomato slices in concentric circles around dough. Sprinkle with pepper and olive oil.

Bake uncovered for 20 to 25 minutes until cheese is lightly golden around edges and crust is brown. Sprinkle with basil. Serve warm.

Makes 4 servings.

Test kitchen notes: Vary the vegetables by using red peppers, onions, mushrooms or spinach. Roma tomatoes are small and oblong and usually contain less juice than ordinary red tomatoes.

Nutrition information per serving: calories, 337; fat, 14.1 grams; carbohydrate, 39.6 grams; cholesterol, 25 milligrams; sodium, 367 milligrams.

Pizza toppings

Oyster mushrooms
Goat cheese
Broccoli
Spinach
Water chestnuts
Sun-dried tomatoes (not packed in oil)
Fennel
Fresh sage
Turkey sausage
Smoked salmon

■ This pizza explodes with the colors and flavors of summer. It can be a full meal or a beautiful first course for a dinner party.

Artichoke and Pepper Pizza

1 (10-ounce) package frozen
   artichoke hearts, thawed
Lemon juice
1 medium green pepper, thinly
   sliced (about 1½ cups)
½ medium red pepper, thinly
   sliced (about ¾ cup)
1 small onion, sliced vertically
   (about 1 cup)
1 clove garlic, minced
2 tablespoons olive oil
½ teaspoon oregano, crushed
Salt and pepper to taste
1½ cups (about 6 ounces)
   shredded mozzarella cheese
3 tablespoons grated
Parmesan cheese

Pizza dough:
1 cup plus 2 tablespoons flour
½ cup whole-wheat flour
1 package active dry yeast
½ teaspoon thyme
½ teaspoon salt
½ cup warm water (120 F)
1 tablespoon olive oil

Cut artichokes in half. In a non-stick skillet, saute artichokes 5 minutes in lemon juice until the liquid has evaporated. Add peppers, onion and garlic and saute 5 minutes longer or until vegetables are tender. Sprinkle with oregano.

To prepare pizza dough, combine white flour and ½ cup whole wheat flour, yeast and ½ teaspoon each thyme and salt in a mixing bowl.

Add ½ cup warm water (120 F) and 1 tablespoon olive oil; beat with electric mixer until smooth. Knead until smooth and elastic. Cover; let rise 30 minutes.

Shape pizza dough into a 12-inch circle on an ungreased pizza pan or pizza stone. Sprinkle dough with mozzarella. Add artichoke mixture. Season to taste with salt and pepper. Top with Parmesan cheese. Bake at 450 F for 15 to 20 minutes.

Makes 1 (12-inch) pizza or 4 servings.

Test kitchen notes: For a variation, substitute 1 loaf of frozen bread dough, thawed, for pizza dough and substitute 8 ounces of ricotta cheese seasoned with 2 cloves of garlic for the mozzarella cheese.

Nutrition information per serving: calories, 471; fat, 21.5 grams; carbohydrate, 52.4 grams; cholesterol, 36 milligrams; sodium, 572 milligrams.

Rolled instead of flat, this extraordinary lasagna combines the mellow richness of ricotta cheese with an extra zesty Marinara Sauce.

Fresh Spinach and Ricotta Lasagna

1 pound fresh lasagna noodles
1 pound frozen chopped spinach, thawed or 14 ounces fresh spinach, washed
3 tablespoons Parmesan cheese, grated
2 cups part-skim ricotta cheese
¼ teaspoon ground nutmeg
¼ teaspoon dried basil, crumbled
4 drops hot pepper sauce
1 teaspoon anchovy paste (optional)
Non-stick cooking spray
Salt and pepper to taste (optional)
Marinara Sauce (recipe follows)

Keep lasagna noodles moist in warm water while preparing filling.

Preheat oven to 325 F.

If using frozen spinach, drain and squeeze out excess liquid. If using fresh spinach, chop finely and put in a non-stick pan with tightfitting lid.

Wilt spinach over medium-high heat for 3 minutes. Drain, cool and squeeze out excess liquid. In a bowl, combine spinach with Parmesan cheese, ricotta, nutmeg, basil, anchovy paste and hot pepper sauce. Season with salt and pepper to taste, if desired.

Coat a baking dish with non-stick cooking spray; set aside. Drain noodles and spread spinach-ricotta mixture thinly along length of each. Roll noodles, pinwheel-style, and place each upright in a baking dish. (Secure with a toothpick, if necessary.) Cover and bake for 15 to 20 minutes until hot. Pour ¼ cup of hot Marinara Sauce over each roll. Bake 10 minutes longer.

Serve 2 rolls per person with extra sauce on the side.

Makes 4 servings.

Test kitchen notes: Fresh lasagna noodles are available by special order at some pasta shops, Italian grocery stores and restaurants. Dip fresh noodles in boiling water for about 1 minute to cook them before rolling.

Serve with a green, steamed vegetable such as snow peas, broccoli or zucchini squash.

Nutrition information per serving: calories, 62; fat, 3.43 grams; carbohydrate, 7.5 grams; cholesterol, 0 milligrams; sodium, 546 milligrams.

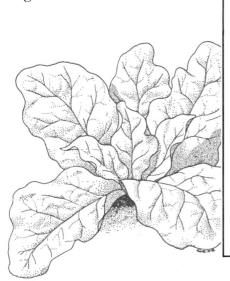

Pasta facts

■ Pasta is a combination of flour made from hard durum wheat, water and salt. Noodles usually contain eggs as well.

■ Pasta dough is kneaded and rolled until it is thin and hard. It can be cut into almost any shape. If prepared while the dough is moist and pliable, it is considered fresh pasta. Fresh pasta cooks in about a minute in boiling, salted water.

■ If dried until it is rigid, pasta cooks in about 5 to 10 minutes depending on size and thickness.

■ Rinse cooked pasta briefly in hot water after cooking. Serve immediately.

Marinara Sauce

2 tablespoons olive oil

2 small yellow onions, chopped

2 cloves garlic, minced or crushed in a garlic press

1 (28-ounce) can peeled Italian plum tomatoes

¼ teaspoon dried oregano

¼ teaspoon dried sage or basil

¼ teaspoon dried thyme

1 teaspoon firmly packed brown sugar

¼ teaspoon salt

¼ teaspoon freshly ground black pepper

1 tablespoon Worcestershire sauce

Heat oil in a saucepan. Saute onions until limp and transparent. Add garlic and entire contents of canned tomatoes. Crush tomatoes with a spoon. Add oregano, salt, pepper and Worcestershire sauce and simmer for 20 minutes. If desired, puree sauce in a blender or food processor and strain. Serve hot over lasagna.

Makes 8 servings or 2½ cups.

Nutrition information per serving: calories, 62; fat, 3.43 grams; carbohydrate, 7.5 grams; cholesterol, 0 milligrams; sodium, 546 milligrams.

■ Experienced cooks may want to make homemade ravioli but fresh commercial ravioli is available in the refrigerated foods section of most grocery stores.

Cheese Ravioli
With Tomato and Red Bell Pepper Sauce

2 pounds fresh, jumbo cheese or spinach ravioli (about 24)

2 tablespoons olive oil

½ onion, chopped

2 cloves garlic, chopped

2 large sweet red peppers, chopped

3 ripe tomatoes

¼ teaspoon salt

1 tablespoon balsamic vinegar

4 leaves fresh basil, sliced into strips

Heat olive oil in a separate saucepan and add the chopped onion. Saute until soft. Add the garlic and chopped peppers and tomatoes. Cover the saucepan and reduce the heat to low. Stew the vegetables until soft, about 10 to 12 minutes. Add the salt and balsamic vinegar. Pour vegetables into a food processor, food mill or blender and process until smooth.

For a smooth, velvety sauce, press the mixture through a strainer. Sauce is fine served as is, however.

Meanwhile, cook the ravioli for about 5 minutes in boiling water until just tender; drain.

Pour red pepper sauce on the plate and arrange ravioli on top. Garnish with fresh basil.

Serve immediately.

Makes 6 servings.

Nutrition information per serving using cheese ravioli: calories, 429; fat, 21.2 grams; carbohydrate, 69.5 grams; cholesterol, 48.3 milligrams; sodium, 747 milligrams.

■ Nutty-tasting sesame seed paste with a dash of chili and ginger give this cool pasta salad extra zip.

Oriental-Style Chilled Noodle Salad in Sesame Sauce

3 tablespoons chicken broth or hot water

2 tablespoons sesame seed paste (tahini) or smooth peanut butter

1 tablespoon low-sodium soy sauce

1 teaspoon fresh ginger, grated or finely chopped

1 clove fresh garlic, minced

⅛ teaspoon ground red chili or cayenne pepper

1 teaspoon Oriental sesame oil

½ pound cooked, chilled rice vermicelli or thin spaghetti

1 cup bean sprouts

¼ cup green onions, chopped

2 tablespoons fresh cilantro or parsley, chopped

2 tablespoons roasted, unsalted peanuts, chopped

In a microwave-safe dish or a small saucepan, combine broth or water, sesame seed paste or peanut butter, soy sauce, ginger, garlic and red chili. Cook in a microwave oven on high power (100 percent) until mixture bubbles and becomes fragrant, about 2 minutes, stirring at 30-second intervals. Remove from heat and stir in sesame oil. Chill dressing until ready to serve.

In a large bowl, combine cooked rice vermicelli or spaghetti and bean sprouts. Toss to combine. Add dressing and toss, coating noodles thoroughly. Transfer to a serving platter or individual plates.

Garnish with chopped green onions, cilantro or parsley and chopped peanuts.

Makes 4 servings.

Nutrition information per serving: calories, 200; fat, 8 grams; carbohydrate, 25.3 grams; cholesterol, 0 milligrams; sodium, 163 milligrams.

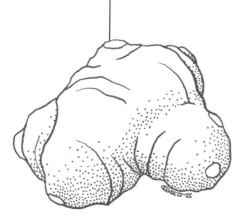

■ The superb flavors of lemon, garlic and a mellow Italian blue cheese called Gorgonzola, create a moist, delectable stuffing for artichokes.

Stuffed Italian Artichokes

4 large artichokes

Juice of ½ lemon (about 3 tablespoons)

¼ cup water

½ teaspoon lemon zest

1 cup bread crumbs (about 2 slices)

1 tablespoon olive oil

1 clove garlic, crushed through a press

½ cup fresh zucchini, grated (about 1 small zucchini)

1 ounce Gorgonzola cheese (Italian blue cheese or substitute domestic blue cheese)

½ cup part-skim mozzarella, grated

¼ teaspoon salt

¼ teaspoon freshly ground black pepper

½ teaspoon marjoram or oregano, crushed

½ teaspoon basil, crushed

Trim off the artichoke stems, cutting them flush with the bottom so that artichokes will stand upright. Peel stems and reserve. Rub bottom of the artichokes with lemon. Cut about ½ inch off the top of the artichoke and rub surface with lemon. Using kitchen shears, snip off the thorns on the tops of remaining leaves. Squeeze lemon juice over top of artichokes.

Place the artichokes in the microwave oven in a microwave-safe baking dish. Add the water and reserved stems. Cover well and cook on high power (100 percent) for 14 to 16 minutes, rotating dish every 4 minutes. Artichokes are done when a leaf in the center pulls out easily and bottom is tender. Discard water. Chop stems and set aside. Allow artichokes to stand 5 minutes.

(If you do not have a microwave oven, trim the artichokes as directed. Bring a kettle of salted water to a boil and cook the artichokes until bottoms are tender, about 15 to 20 minutes. Drain artichokes upside down, until cool enough to handle.)

Flavors that accent artichokes

■ Basil
■ Rosemary
■ Shallots
■ Leeks
■ Blue cheese
■ Balsamic vinegar

Prepare the stuffing by combining lemon zest, bread crumbs, oil, garlic, zucchini, Gorgonzola and mozzarella cheeses and seasonings. Mash to combine thoroughly. Add chopped, reserved artichoke stems. Mixture should be moist but not mushy.

When artichokes are cool enough to handle, spread the center leaves apart. Pull out the stiff, purplish leaves at the cores. Using a spoon, scrape out the fuzzy hairs of the chokes. Place about 2 to 3 tablespoons of filling in the cavity of each artichoke and about 1 teaspoon between the outer leaves.

To finish artichokes in a conventional oven, bake at 400 F for 10 to 12 minutes. Serve warm.

Makes 4 servings.

Test kitchen notes: Served with a green salad or a fresh fruit salad, this makes a complete meal. The artichokes may also be served as appetizers. As appetizers, the dish will serve 10.

Nutrition information per serving: calories, 166; fat, 8.1 grams; carbohydrate, 17.8 grams; cholesterol, 14 milligrams; sodium, 424 milligrams.

■Warm and satisfying, this peasant-style pasta and bean soup is high in complex carbohydrates and low in fat.

Pasta e Fagioli (Pasta and Bean Soup)

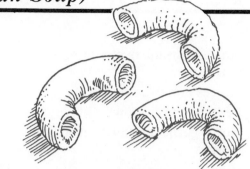

2 quarts water

4 ounces (1 cup) pasta, such as rigatoni, small shells or elbow macaroni

1 medium onion, chopped

1 tablespoon olive oil

2 cloves garlic, minced

2 cups canned Italian plum tomatoes, coarsely chopped, with juice

1 tablespoon tomato paste

2 tablespoons fresh basil, chopped, or ½ teaspoon dried

¼ teaspoon dried rosemary

¼ teaspoon salt

¼ teaspoon freshly ground black pepper

⅛ teaspoon crushed red pepper (optional)

1 (14-ounce) can Italian cannelini beans, with juice

¼ cup freshly grated Parmesan or Romano cheese

4 teaspoons parsley, chopped

Bring water to a boil in a deep kettle. Cook the pasta until al dente and drain. Rinse pasta with hot water and set aside.

In a saucepan or a deep microwave-safe casserole, heat oil and cook onion until soft and transparent. Add garlic and cook until fragrant. Stir in chopped tomatoes, tomato paste, basil, rosemary, salt, black pepper and optional red pepper. Cover and simmer for 20 minutes on the stovetop or about 12 minutes in a microwave oven on high power (100 percent). Add the cannelini beans and juice. Cook mixture for about 10 minutes longer on the stovetop or 2 minutes on high in the microwave oven.

Spoon the pasta into 4 serving bowls and spoon the bean and tomato mixture with broth on top. Sprinkle with cheese and parsley. Serve warm.

Makes 4 servings.

Nutrition information per serving: calories, 327; fat, 6.1 grams; carbohydrate, 53.3 grams; cholesterol, 4 milligrams; sodium, 401 milligrams.

■ Several Florida mushrooms growers produce exotic oyster, crimini and shiitake mushrooms, so they are often available in grocery stores and produce markets.

Pasta With Fresh Exotic Mushrooms

8 ounces crimini, oyster or shiitake mushrooms

8 ounces domestic mushrooms

1 tablespoon olive oil

2 cloves garlic, crushed through a press

2 shallots, minced

⅓ cup dry Marsala

¼ cup water or chicken broth

1 tablespoon soy sauce

3 tablespoons balsamic or red-wine vinegar

1 teaspoon dried rosemary crushed

½ teaspoon salt

2 tablespoons parsley, chopped

2 tablespoons fresh basil, chopped

12 ounces dried or 9 ounces fresh spinach fettuccine

¼ cup Parmesan cheese, grated

Freshly grated black pepper

Wipe mushrooms clean with a damp cloth or paper towel. Cut into ¼-inch slices.

Heat olive oil over medium heat in large, non-stick skillet. Add the crimini, oyster or shiitake mushrooms. Cook, stirring frequently for 6 to 8 minutes, until mushrooms have rendered their juices and are dark brown. Add the domestic mushrooms. Continue cooking for 3 minutes longer, until mushrooms begin to lose their moisture.

Add the garlic and shallots to the pan. Cook for 2 minutes, stirring. Add the Marsala wine, water, soy sauce, vinegar, rosemary and salt. Bring liquid to a simmer. Add parsley and basil and remove from heat.

Bring a kettle of salted water to a boil. Cook the fettuccine according to package instructions. Drain thoroughly and empty into a large bowl. Pour the mushroom mixture over pasta and toss to coat every strand. Pepper to taste.

Divide into 4 portions and sprinkle with Parmesan cheese.

Makes 4 servings.

Test kitchen notes: Crimini mushrooms, also called brown, Roman or field mushrooms, are dark-brown relatives of the ordinary button mushroom. They are larger and have a most pronounced flavor. Oyster mushrooms, called pleurottes in French cooking, have an almost seafood-like flavor. Shiitake mushrooms have large, flat caps, a woody odor, a rich mushroom flavor and a meaty texture.

Nutrition information per serving: calories, 424; fat, 6.4 grams; carbohydrate, 70.9 grams; cholesterol, 4 milligrams; sodium, 497 milligrams.

■ If you have been looking for a vegetarian entree the whole family will love, risotto is the answer. Be sure to buy Arborio rice for the authentic creamy consistency.

Garlic and Lemon Risotto With Olives

6 cups water

½ teaspoon salt

1 head garlic, unpeeled and coarsely chopped

1 tablespoon olive oil

1 small onion or 2 shallots, chopped

2 cloves garlic, peeled and crushed through a press

1 cup Arborio rice, rinsed under cold running water

¼ cup dry white wine

⅛ teaspoon white pepper

Juice of ½ lemon (2 to 3 tablespoons)

1 teaspoon lemon zest, freshly grated

¼ cup Parmesan cheese, freshly grated

½ cup black or green olives, preferably Italian, French or Greek

In a large saucepan, bring water, salt and all but 2 cloves of garlic to a boil. Reduce heat, cover and simmer for 20 minutes. Remove and discard garlic. Reserve 4 cups of garlic water.

Heat the oil in the saucepan. Add the onion or shallots. Cook, stirring frequently, until vegetables are transparent, about 3 minutes. Add the remaining garlic and the rice to the saucepan, stirring to coat every grain with oil.

Stir in the white wine and adjust heat so it bubbles but does not evaporate too quickly. Add 1 cup of the garlic water to the rice. Stir frequently to keep rice from sticking to pan and to keep liquid distributed. Continue stirring and adding the garlic water by cupfuls until there is only ½ cup left, about 20 to 25 minutes. Rice should be creamy-looking but tender.

Pit the olives if necessary and cut into halves.

Stir the white pepper, lemon juice and lemon zest into the remaining ½ cup of

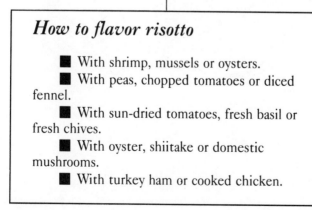

How to flavor risotto

■ With shrimp, mussels or oysters.
■ With peas, chopped tomatoes or diced fennel.
■ With sun-dried tomatoes, fresh basil or fresh chives.
■ With oyster, shiitake or domestic mushrooms.
■ With turkey ham or cooked chicken.

garlic water. Stir mixture into the rice and cook for 1 to 2 more minutes. Add half of the Parmesan cheese and the olives and stir again. Remove from heat and serve immediately, sprinkled with remaining cheese.

Makes 4 servings.

Test Kitchen notes: Arborio is a short-grained Italian rice that can absorb a great deal of liquid without falling apart or getting mushy. Risotto is a specialty of Venice, where the dish is served with a variety of foods, including seafood, mushrooms, sausage, ham and vegetables. This meatless version works well as a main course with a salad, such as Tosssed Vegetables With Pecan Dressing (page 34) or Strawberry-Avocado Salad (page 26).

Nutrition information per serving: calories, 224; fat, 6.3 grams; carbohydrate, 34.7 grams; cholesterol, 4 milligrams; sodium, 925 milligrams.

■ Few dishes are more quintessentially Cuban than black beans. This hearty combination is served as a side dish in restaurants, but it can be a complete meal at home.

Black Beans and Rice

1 pound dried black beans

6 cups water

2 tablespoons olive oil

2 medium onions, peeled and chopped

6 cloves garlic, crushed through a press

2 bay leaves

1 whole dried red chili pod (optional)

¼ teaspoon cumin

¼ teaspoon dried oregano

1 teaspoon salt

½ teaspoon freshly ground black pepper

2 tablespoons dry wine or sherry

1½ tablespoons apple-cider vinegar

1 teaspoon sugar

½ cup white onion, chopped for garnishing

2 cups hot, cooked white rice

Hot sauce (optional)

Pick over the beans, discarding any shriveled ones. Place in a colander and wash several times under running water.

Place in a large kettle and cover with water. Soak overnight.

The following day, drain the beans and rinse in fresh water. Replace with 6 cups fresh water. Place kettle over high heat and bring water to a boil. Reduce heat to a slow simmer. Cook for 45 minutes.

In a separate saucepan, combine olive oil and 2 chopped onions. Cook over medium heat until onions are transparent, about 3 minutes. Add garlic and cook for 2 minutes longer. To the onion mixture add bay leaves and optional chili pod and simmer for 45 minutes longer. Add onion mixture to beans.

The beans can be prepared ahead to this point. Store, covered, in the refrigerator. When ready to finish cooking, reheat the beans to a simmer and prepare the rice.

Add the cumin, oregano, salt, pepper, sherry, vinegar and sugar to the beans. Simmer another 30 to 40 minutes until beans are tender but not mushy. Add another ½ to 1 cup of water if necessary. Remove bay leaf and chili pod.

Serve 1 cup of beans per person and garnish with a sprinkling of chopped onion. Serve with ¼ cup of white rice. Sprinkle with hot sauce if desired.

Makes 8 servings.

Nutrition information per serving: calories, 298; fat, 4.3 grams; carbohydrate, 52.2 grams; cholesterol, 0 milligrams; sodium, 489 milligrams.

SIDE DISHES

Skinny Guacamole

1 ripe avocado, peeled and
   seeded
1 green onion, chopped
1 small ripe tomato, seeded and
   chopped
1/4 teaspoon salt
1/2 teaspoon black pepper
1 1/2 tablespoons lime juice
2 tablespoons fresh cilantro,
   finely chopped
2 drops hot pepper sauce

Chop avocado. Combine avocado, green onion, tomato, salt, pepper, lime juice, cilantro and hot pepper sauce. Stir and mash slightly to blend. Serve at room temperature. Makes 1 cup.

Nutrition information per serving: calories, 93; fat, 7.8 grams; carbohydrate, 6.6 grams; cholesterol, 0 milligrams; sodium, 164 milligrams.

Fast facts

■ Florida avocados are not only larger than California varieties, but they have smoother, lighter colored skins than their California counterparts.

■ Florida avocados contain between 3 and 15 percent fat while California avocados contain between 15 and 30 percent fat. Dietitians recommend eating avocados — either Florida or California — no more than once a week.

■ These flavorful patties make a wonderful side dish for brunch or dinner. Serve with egg dishes or broiled, lean beef.

Mushroom Pancakes

1 pound mushrooms with stems (use domestic, crimini or shiitake)
2 egg whites
2 green onions, minced
1 tablespoon flour
3 tablespoons cracker crumbs
½ teaspoon salt
¼ teaspoon pepper
3 tablespoons olive oil
1 tablespoon soy sauce
1 teaspoon freshly grated ginger

Place the mushrooms in a food processor or blender. Chop until mushrooms are the size of rice grains.

Empty mushrooms into a strainer. Using a spatula, press the mushrooms against the wall of the strainer to press out most of the liquid.

Combine the egg whites, onions, flour, cracker crumbs, salt, pepper, olive oil, soy sauce and ginger to make thick batter. Stir into the mushrooms.

Drop the mushroom batter by ¼-cupfuls into a non-stick skillet or griddle.

Cook over medium heat for 5 minutes, turning once, until pancakes are browned and set.

Makes 8 servings.

Test kitchen notes: Serve these meaty, richly flavored pancakes for brunch with an omelette or as a dinner side dish with roasted meats or grilled chicken.

Nutrition information per serving: calories, 95; fat, 6.8 grams; carbohydrate, 6.6 grams; cholesterol, 43 milligrams; sodium, 224 milligrams.

■Chevre is a French term for any soft, goat-milk cheese. These cheeses have a distinctive tang that makes them excellent for cooking. Goat's milk is lower in fat than cow's milk.

Chevre-Stuffed Tomatoes

2 ripe, firm large tomatoes, sliced in half horizontally (or 4 small tomatoes, cored and left whole)

1 green onion, minced

1 teaspoon olive oil

¼ teaspoon salt

¼ teaspoon basil, crumbled

⅛ teaspoon freshly ground black pepper

2 slices whole-wheat toast, crumbled

3 ounces soft, mild chevre (goat cheese), such as Montrachet

Scoop the seeds and pulp out of the tomatoes, leaving just the thick, meaty shell. Turn tomatoes upside down and allow to drain. Squeeze pulp to remove seeds. Combine pulp in a bowl with green onion, oil, salt, pepper, basil, whole-wheat toast and chevre. Mix thoroughly. Stuff filling into tomato shells. Bake at 425 F for 5 minutes. Turn oven to broiler setting and place tomatoes as close as possible to the heat element. Broil for 1 minute. Serve hot.

Makes 4 servings.

Test kitchen notes: The tomatoes can be prepared in a microwave oven. Bake on medium (50 percent) power for 4 minutes, turning once. Allow to stand 1 minute before serving.

Nutrition information per serving: calories, 144; fat, 8.5 grams; carbohydrate, 11.2 grams; cholesterol, 21 milligrams; sodium, 786 milligrams.

■ These delicious pancakes are baked rather than fried so they absorb a minimum of oil during cooking. Serve them for breakfast or as a side dish instead of rice or pasta.

Potato Pancakes

2 potatoes, grated
1 small onion, finely chopped
2 egg whites
2 tablespoons flour
1 teaspoon lemon juice
½ teaspoon salt
¼ teaspoon black pepper
2 tablespoons peanut oil
Non-stick cooking spray

Preheat oven to 350 F.

Rinse grated potato in cold water to remove starch. Drain thoroughly, squeezing to remove excess moisture. In a large bowl, combine potato, egg whites, flour, lemon juice, onion, salt and pepper; mix well. Pat mixture into cakes.

Heat a non-stick frying pan or griddle. Using a small amount of peanut oil, fry each pancake for about 2 minutes each side, or until lightly browned.

Transfer to a baking sheet that has been sprayed with non-stick spray. Bake for 15 minutes, then turn and bake 10 minutes longer. Serve hot with corn relish.

Makes 8 pancakes.

Nutrition information per pancake: calories, 80; fat, 3.5 grams; carbohydrate, 10.4 grams; cholesterol, 0 milligrams; sodium, 162 milligrams.

A microwave oven cooks this luscious custard quickly. The green chili adds a spicy flavor but the dish isn't too hot.

Eggplant Flan With Green Chili and Cheese

1 large or 2 medium-size eggplants

½ cup water

2 egg whites

1 small onion, chopped

2 cloves garlic, crushed in a press

2 cups whole-wheat bread crumbs (about 3 slices)

½ teaspoon salt

½ teaspoon oregano, crushed

¼ teaspoon black pepper

¼ teaspoon paprika

¼ teaspoon cumin

½ cup green chilies, peeled and chopped or 1 (4-ounce) can diced green chilies, drained

1 cup low-fat Cheddar cheese, grated

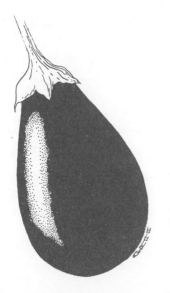

Cut eggplants in cubes to make about 4 cups. Combine with water in a microwave-safe baking dish. Cover with waxed paper and microwave on high (100 percent) power for 5 minutes. Stir and cook for 4 minutes more. Allow to stand 5 minutes. Drain and mash eggplant in a food processor or blender.

Combine eggplant with egg whites, onion, garlic, bread crumbs, salt, pepper, oregano, paprika, cumin and chilies; mix well. Spoon mixture into a casserole or microwave-safe baking dish.

Cover with waxed paper and cook on medium-high (60 percent) power for 5 minutes. Sprinkle with cheese. Cook for 4 minutes longer. Casserole is done when a toothpick comes out clean. If a brown, crusty top is desired, cook under the oven broiler for 2 minutes or until bubbly.

Makes 6 servings.

Test kitchen notes: The casserole can be prepared in advance up to the point that the cheese is added. Reheat in a microwave oven for 4 minutes on medium-high power (60 percent.)

Nutrition information per serving: calories, 114; fat, 3.1 grams; carbohydrate, 16.3 grams; cholesterol, 10 milligrams; sodium, 509 milligrams.

■ Fresh artichokes with raspberry vinegar is a heavenly flavor combination. Artichokes offer a whopping 5 grams of fiber in just 3 ounces, almost twice as much as broccoli or cauliflower.

Artichokes With Raspberry Herb Vinaigrette

6 large artichokes
Juice of 1 large lemon
1 clove of garlic, peeled
½ teaspoon salt

Rinse artichokes and pull off tough outer leaves. Trim stem so that artichokes will sit flat. Use kitchen shears to snip leaves with thorns. Trim top of artichokes so all leaves are flat. Rub cut surfaces with lemon.

Stand artichokes upright in a deep kettle (do not use an aluminum pan because it will cause discoloration). Cover with boiling water. Add remaining lemon juice, the garlic and salt. Bring to a boil. Simmer for 20 minutes, until inside leaves pull out easily. Discard cooking water. Turn artichokes upside down to drain.

Gently spread leaves apart to remove choke. Scoop fuzzy choke out with a spoon.

When ready to serve, dip leaves in Raspberry Herb Vinaigrette.

Makes 6 servings.

Test kitchen notes: The artichokes can be cooked in a microwave oven. Trim and pare as called for in the recipe. Instead of cooking in water, place artichokes right side up in a microwave safe baking dish. Place ¼ cup of water in bottom. Add garlic and salt. Cover with a similar-sized dish. Cook on high power for 5 minutes. Turn dish. Cook on high for 5 minutes. Turn dish again and cook for 3 to 5 minutes longer. Artichokes are done when inside leaves pull out easily.

Nutrition information per serving of plain artichoke: calories, 66 fat, 0.2 gram; carbohydrate, 15.6 grams; cholesterol, 0 milligrams; sodium, 295 milligrams.

Raspberry Herb Vinaigrette

¼ cup raspberry vinegar

1 tablespoon cholesterol-free
  mayonnaise

1 clove garlic, crushed through a
  press

2 teaspoons onion, grated

1 tablespoon fresh tarragon or 1
  teaspoon dried and crushed

1 tablespoon fresh chervil or 1
  teaspoon dried and crushed

¼ teaspoon dry mustard

¼ teaspoon salt

¼ teaspoon freshly ground black
  pepper

¼ cup olive oil

Step 1: Measure first 7 ingredients into a small glass bowl or 1-cup measuring cup.

Combine the vinegar, mayonnaise, garlic, grated onion, herbs and dry mustard. Add salt and pepper and blend well with a fork or small whisk. Add olive oil and stir again.

Makes ¾ cup.

Nutrition information per tablespoon: calories, 46; fat, 5.1 grams; carbohydrate, 0.4 gram; cholesterol, 0 milligrams; sodium, 53 milligrams.

Step 2: Add salt and freshly ground pepper and stir until salt is dissolved in the vinegar.

Step 3: Add olive oil and beat vigorously to mix and thicken.

■ A touch of brown sugar heightens the natural sweetness of the vegetables.

Glazed Carrots and Parsnips

2 pounds parsnips, peeled and
  sliced into 3½-by-½-inch sticks
8 ounces carrots, peeled and cut
  into 3½-by-½-inch sticks
1 cup diced onions
4 cups water
2 teaspoons salt
½ teaspoon pepper
1 tablespoon olive oil or canola
  oil
2 tablespoons firmly packed
  brown sugar
1 tablespoon chopped fresh
  Italian parsley for garnish

In a 12-inch skillet combine vegetables; add water, salt, and pepper and bring mixture to a full boil. Reduce heat, cover, and let simmer until vegetables are tender, 10 to 12 minutes. Drain vegetables; transfer to large bowl and set aside.

In same skillet, heat olive oil or canola oil; stir in brown sugar and cook over medium heat, stirring constantly, until sugar is melted. Add vegetables and cook over medium-high heat until liquid evaporates and vegetables are glazed, about 3 minutes. Transfer to serving dish and sprinkle with parsley.

Makes 4 servings.

Nutrition information per serving: calories, 164; sodium, 1,269 milligrams; fat, 3.6 grams; carbohydrate, 31.8 grams.

■ The ancient Incas called quinoa "the mother grain." Modern dietitians agree that this light, pellet-shaped grain is high in protein and complex carbohydrates but low in fat. Shop for it in health-food stores.

Quinoa Pilaf

2 tablespoons minced onion

2 tablespoons finely diced celery

2 tablespoons finely diced carrot

1½ tablespoons peanut oil

1 cup quinoa, rinsed well

2 cups vegetable or chicken stock, heated

Salt to taste

Pepper to taste

¼ cup golden raisins

¼ cup toasted almonds or pine nuts

In a heavy 2-quart saucepan, saute the onion, celery and carrot in the oil over moderate heat until softened. Add the quinoa and stir until it separates into grains. Add the heated stock, salt and pepper. Stir briefly and reduce the heat so that the liquid simmers. Add the raisins; cover. Cook for 15 minutes until the quinoa has absorbed all of the liquid.

Fluff with a fork; stir in toasted nuts.

Serve with chicken, broiled fish or meatloaf.

Makes 4 servings.

Test kitchen notes: Quinoa has more protein than any other grain. It is considered a complete protein because it has all eight essential amino acids. Tiny and bead-shaped, the ivory-colored quinoa cooks like rice (but takes half the time) and expands to four times its original volume. Unseasoned, the flavor is delicate and almost bland.

Nutrition information per serving: calories, 228; fat, 42.6 grams; carbohydrate, 54.5 grams; cholesterol, 0 milligrams; sodium, 423 milligrams.

Gifts from the granary

Barley: The most common form is pearl barley, which has been partially polished to remove the tough outer bran. It cooks in 30 minutes. Barley has a bland flavor and a soft texture. It is best used in soups, pilafs and casseroles.

Bulgur: Wheat that has been cracked, steamed and dried. It only requires soaking in hot water or broth to prepare. Bulgur has a nutty flavor and chewy texture. It is best used in salads, such as tabouli, casseroles or in meat dishes, such as kibbe.

Couscous: Semolina flour that has been mixed with water to form tiny pellets, like pasta. It requires only soaking in hot water or broth, or steaming over aromatic liquid to prepare. Couscous has a mild flavor and a soft texture. It is best used in salads, pilafs, stuffings, baked foods, soups or side dishes.

Groats: Buckwheat seeds that have been hulled and coarsely cracked. It cooks in about 12 to 15 minutes. It is best used in pilafs, soups, stuffings and side dishes.

Kasha: Cracked buckwheat groats that have been toasted to a reddish-brown color. It has a toasty, nutty flavor and aroma and a fluffy texture. Kasha cooks in about 15 to 20 minutes. It is best used in pilafs, side dishes, soups, stuffings and puddings.

Millet: Tiny hulled grains that look like bird seed. The grains cook in about 30 minutes. Millet has a slightly bitter flavor and a chewy texture. It is best used in stuffings, side dishes, croquettes, baked foods, or meat dishes, such as fish cakes or meatballs.

Quinoa: Whole grains that resemble sesame seeds. Quinoa has a mild flavor with a slightly bitter aftertaste and a springy texture. It must be rinsed in cold, running water before cooking. Quinoa cooks in about 15 minutes. It is best used in side dishes, soups, stuffings, stews and baked goods.

This chunky, all-vegetable spread is used in Mexico instead of fat-laden butter or margarine.

Mantequilla de Pobre (Poor Man's Butter)

4 tomatoes, finely diced
4 ripe California avocados or 2 ripe Florida avocados, finely diced
1½ teaspoons salt
2 tablespoons fresh cilantro, chopped
2 tablespoons vegetable oil
3 tablespoons red-wine vinegar
Unsalted tortilla chips dipping

Mix chopped ingredients well. Add salt, cilantro, oil and vinegar. Taste for seasonings. Chill 1 hour. Serve as a dip with tortilla chips or use as a spread for New Mexican Blue Corn Muffins (page 164).

Makes 12 servings.

Test kitchen notes: Don't mash avocado or puree in a food processor or mixture will resemble guacamole.

Nutrition information per serving: calories, 137; fat, 12.6 grams; carbohydrate, 7.3 grams; cholesterol, 0 milligrams; sodium, 303 milligrams.

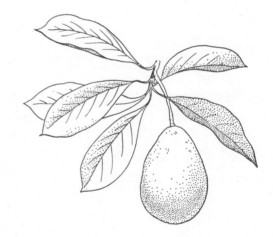

■ Fresh cilantro is a peppery herb that is often available in the produce section of most grocery stores. Though cilantro looks like Italian parsley, it is always sold with the roots attached.

Fresh Salsa

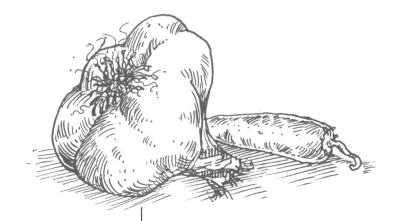

4 to 6 jalapeno chilies (for milder salsa, substitute 2 cans green chilies)
1 medium onion
2 green onions
2 large ripe tomatoes
2 cloves garlic
½ cup fresh cilantro
½ teaspoon ground cumin
¼ cup olive oil
¼ cup red-wine vinegar
Dash of Worcestershire sauce
½ teaspoon salt
Freshly ground black pepper

Wearing rubber gloves, cut off the stems of the jalapenos and remove the seeds. Mince and combine in a bowl.

Finely chop the onion, green onions and tomatoes and cilantro and add to the jalapenos. Add remaining ingredients and refrigerate until serving.

Makes about 2 cups.

Test kitchen notes: Fresh cilantro can be purchased in most supermarkets. Ask the produce manager about its availability.

This recipe can be made up to 3 days in advance, as it improves with age.

Nutrition information per ½ cup: calories, 154; fat, 13.8 grams; carbohydrate, 8.3 grams; cholesterol, 0 milligrams; sodium, 301 milligrams.

■ Serve this warm version of fruit-and-cheese as a side dish in place of a vegetable or a bread.

Broiled Pears with Gorgonzola Cheese

2 ripe red Bartlett or Bosc pears
2 ounces Gorgonzola cheese or
  blue cheese, crumbled

Halve pears lengthwise. Core. If necessary, slice a small bit off the bottom of each half so pear will sit without rolling. Divide cheese over pears. Broil 4 inches from heating element for about 3 minutes, until cheese is soft and melted and pear is slightly blistered. Serve warm.

Makes 4 servings.

Test kitchen notes: This combination is a delicious surprise and ideal for fall when pears are in season and inexpensive.

Nutrition information per serving: calories, 99; fat, 4.4 grams; carbohydrate, 12.8 grams; cholesterol, 11 milligrams; sodium, 198 milligrams.

■Make this better-than-basic vinegar and olive oil dressing a standard in your kitchen. Use it for any kind of salad, but it also makes an excellent marinade for grilled fish and chicken.

Tomato-Basil Vinaigrette

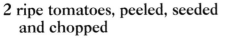

2 ripe tomatoes, peeled, seeded
  and chopped
1 clove garlic
¼ cup olive oil
4 tablespoons fresh basil,
  chopped, or ½ teaspoon dried
  basil
¼ cup balsamic vinegar
½ teaspoon sugar
1 tablespoon whole-grain or
  Dijon-style mustard
¼ teaspoon salt
¼ teaspoon freshly ground black
  pepper

Combine all ingredients in a blender or food processor; mix thoroughly. Allow mixture to stand at least 15 minutes for flavors to blend. Serve at room temperature.

Makes 4 servings.

Nutrition information per serving: calories, 154; fat, 14.1 grams; carbohydrate, 6.9 grams; cholesterol, 0 milligrams; sodium, 266 milligrams.

■ Serve this colorful pilaf instead of white rice.

Red Rice

1¼ cups water
¼ cup tomato sauce
1 tablespoon Worcestershire
    Sauce
¼ teaspoon thyme, crumbled
1 cup rice

Combine water, tomato sauce, Worcestershire sauce and thyme. Bring to a boil. Stir in rice. Reduce heat and simmer for 10 minutes. Turn off heat and allow to stand 10 minutes. Fluff with a fork before serving.

Makes 4 servings.

Nutrition information per serving: calories, 158; fat, 0.1 gram; carbohydrate, 34.8 grams; cholesterol, 0 milligrams; sodium, 631 milligrams.

■ As simple as it is to make, the combination of textures and flavors make this side dish really seem special.

Lentil and Rice Pilaf With Basil

1 teaspoon olive oil

1 small yellow onion, chopped (about ½ cup)

½ teaspoon salt

¼ teaspoon freshly ground black pepper

¼ teaspoon dried basil, crushed

½ cup long-grain white rice

¼ cup short-grain white rice

¼ cup brown lentils, rinsed under running water

2 cups water

2 tablespoons fresh basil, minced

In a saucepan, heat the olive oil and cook the onion until transparent, stirring frequently. Stir in the salt, pepper and dried basil. Stir in the long-grain rice, short-grain rice and lentils. Make sure all the grains are coated with some of the cooking oil. Add the water and bring to a boil. Stir once and reduce heat to a simmer. Cook, loosely covered, for 12 minutes.

Remove from heat. Stir mixture and allow to stand 5 to 6 minutes to plump the grains and absorb any remaining water. Stir in fresh basil just before serving.

Makes 6 servings.

Test kitchen notes: Any herb can be used in place of basil, including rosemary, thyme, oregano or marjoram. If you can't find fresh basil, substitute fresh, minced parsley or the minced tops of green onions.

Nutrition information per serving: calories, 126; fat, 1 gram; carbohydrate, 24.8 grams; cholesterol, 0 milligrams; sodium, 197 milligrams.

■ Most versions of this zesty, garlicky herb sauce contain astronomical amounts of oil, cheese and nuts. You'll never miss the fat in this slimmed-down version.

Low-Fat Pesto Sauce

½ cup fresh parsley

1 bunch fresh basil (about 1 cup, including stems)

½ teaspoon dried basil, crushed

1 tablespoon extra-virgin olive oil

1 tablespoon balsamic or red-wine vinegar

1 to 2 cloves garlic

1 teaspoon light corn syrup

2 tablespoons Parmesan cheese, grated

¼ teaspoon salt

¼ teaspoon freshly ground black pepper

3 tablespoons chicken broth (or more if a thinner sauce is desired)

3 tablespoons walnuts, chopped

Combine parsley and dried and fresh basil in the bowl of a blender or food processor.

Chop finely. While machine is running, add olive oil, vinegar, garlic, cheese, corn syrup, salt, pepper and broth. Puree into a paste. Add walnuts; process until nuts are finely chopped.

Serve at room temperature.

Makes 1 cup.

Test kitchen notes: This Low-Fat Pesto Sauce is an all-purpose condiment that freezes well.

Nutrition information per tablespoon: calories, 27; fat, 2 grams; carbohydrate, 2 grams; cholesterol, 0.5 milligram; sodium, 58 milligrams.

Pass the pesto please

■ Use as a topping for baked sweet or white potatoes.

■ Use instead of butter or margarine on toast, bagels or English muffins.

■ Use as a sauce for pasta.

■ Use as a topping for pizza or crackers.

■ Use as a topping for baked or broiled fish or shellfish.

■ Look for chili oil in the Oriental section of most grocery stores. It is also available in Oriental markets. Just a drop or two will do — it is hot!

Sesame Ginger Dressing

1 clove garlic, minced
1 slice of fresh ginger (about the size of a quarter), minced
1½ tablespoons Oriental sesame oil
¼ cup peanut oil
3 tablespoons soy sauce
1½ teaspoons sugar
3 tablespoons cider or rice-wine vinegar
4 drops Oriental chili oil

Combine all ingredients. Shake vigorously. Allow flavors to blend at room temperature before using.

Makes 8 servings.

Test kitchen notes: Chili oil can be purchased as Asian grocery stores and the ethnic foods section of large grocery stores.

Nutrition information per serving: calories, 90; fat, 9.3 grams; carbohydrate, 1.8 grams; cholesterol, 0 milligrams; sodium, 311 milligrams.

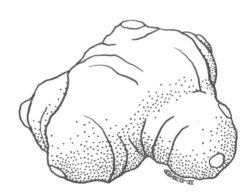

■ Sweet, tart, creamy and delicious, this pineapple dressing could become a favorite with your family.

Creamy Pineapple Dressing

Juice from 1 (8-ounce) can unsweetened pineapple (reserve fruit for another use) or about ⅓ cup
¼ cup apple-cider vinegar
1 teaspoon dry mustard
2 teaspoons lemon juice
½ teaspoon salt
1 teaspoon sugar
1 tablespoon cornstarch
4 tablespoons cholesterol-free mayonnaise

In a small saucepan combine pineapple juice, vinegar, mustard, lemon juice, salt, sugar and cornstarch. Heat over medium-low until thickened, stirring frequently.

Remove from heat and stir in mayonnaise. Chill before using.

Makes 8 servings.

Nutrition information per serving: calories, 47; fat, 3.4 grams; carbohydrate, 4.2 grams; cholesterol, 0 milligrams; sodium, 172 milligrams.

■ French hazelnut oil gives this extraordinary salad a subtle flavor of toasted nuts. Look for the oil in gourmet food stores. If you can't find it, substitute walnut oil or peanut oil.

Lemon and Hazelnut Dressing

3 tablespoons fresh lemon juice
1 tablespoon Dijon-style mustard
½ teaspoon salt
¼ teaspoon white pepper
3 drops hot sauce
3 tablespoons hazelnut oil
2 tablespoons cholesterol-free mayonnaise

In a bowl or a food processor, combine the lemon juice, salt, pepper and hot sauce. Whip until combined. Add the oils and mayonnaise and continue to blend.

Refrigerate until ready to use.

Makes 5 servings.

Nutrition information per recipe: calories, 105; fat, 11 grams; carbohydrate, 2 grams; cholesterol, 0 milligrams; sodium, 343 milligrams.

■Oriental sesame oil is made from toasted sesame seeds and has a dark color, distinct taste and aroma. It adds pizazz to plain white rice.

Sesame Rice

1 teaspoon peanut oil
1 tablespoon sesame seeds
1 cup rice
½ teaspoon salt
1½ cups water
1 teaspoon Oriental sesame oil

Heat the oil in a saucepan over medium-high heat. Add the sesame seeds and toast until lightly browned. Be careful not to burn. Stir in rice and salt. Add the water and sesame oil. Stir.

Cover and bring water to a boil. Reduce heat and simmer for 10 minutes. Turn off heat and allow rice to stand covered until all liquid has been absorbed. Serve in place of plain white rice.

Makes 4 servings.

Test kitchen notes: Sesame oil is never used for frying, but only to add a nutty flavor to dishes. It is available in Oriental markets and in the ethnic food section of most grocery stores.

Nutrition information per serving: calories, 211; fat, 3.7 grams; carbohydrate, 39.6 grams; cholesterol, 0 milligrams; sodium, 295 milligrams.

■ This tangy relish is excellent with mild cheeses, such as cream cheese, Cheddar or Monterey Jack. It is also good as a filling for omelets.

Rhubarb-Apple Chutney

1 tablespoon oil

1 tablespoon fresh ginger, chopped

1 large onion, coarsely chopped

2 cloves garlic, chopped

2 cups rhubarb, chopped

½ cup water

¾ cup sugar

½ cup apple-cider vinegar

1 tart green apple, cored and chopped

1 (1-inch) piece cinnamon stick or ¼ teaspoon ground

1 bay leaf

½ cup raisins

½ teaspoon salt

½ teaspoon pepper

In a large saucepan, heat the oil and saute the ginger until fragrant.

Add the onion, garlic, rhubarb, water, sugar, vinegar, apple, cinnamon, bay leaf, raisins, salt and pepper.

Bring to a boil. Reduce heat to a simmer and cook slowly for 20 minutes.

Mixture should be thick but not soupy.

Pour into sterilized jars and seal or serve at room temperature with grilled fish or chicken, roast pork or duck.

Refrigerate uneaten portion.

Makes 3 cups.

Nutrition information per serving: calories, 94; fat, 1.3 grams; carbohydrate, 21.4 grams; cholesterol, 0 milligrams; sodium, 100 milligrams.

■ Barley is high in soluble fiber and it tastes delicious, too. Red and green pepper add color.

Barley Pilaf

1 tablespoon olive oil
2 green onions, chopped
1 cup quick-cooking barley
2 cups water
¼ teaspoon salt
1 tablespoon balsamic or red-wine vinegar
¼ teaspoon freshly ground black pepper
¼ teaspoon thyme
2 tablespoons red bell pepper, minced
2 tablespoons green bell pepper, minced

In a saucepan over medium-high heat, cook green onion in olive oil. Stir in barley, coating each grain. Add water, salt, vinegar, black pepper and thyme and simmer for 10 to 12 minutes. Stir in red and green pepper. Remove from heat and allow to stand 5 minutes until all liquid is absorbed.

Nutrition information per serving: calories, 205; fat, 3.9 grams; carbohydrate, 39.6 grams; cholesterol, 0 milligrams; sodium, 148 milligrams.

You don't have to give up your favorite foods to follow a low-fat diet. These delicious "fries" aren't fried at all.

Oven-Baked Fries

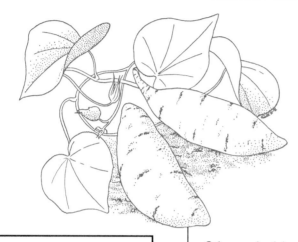

2 large baking potatoes, unpeeled
⅛ teaspoon salt
Non-stick cooking spray or olive
   oil cooking spray

Slice potatoes lengthwise into strips. Cook, covered, in a microwave oven on high (100 percent) power for 5 minutes. Allow to stand for at least 3 minutes or until cool enough to handle.

Preheat oven to 375 F.

Arrange potato slices on a baking sheet. Spray with cooking spray and sprinkle with salt. Bake uncovered for 15 to 20 minutes until crisp and browned along edges. Serve hot.

Makes 4 servings.

Test kitchen notes: This recipe works just as well using peeled sweet potatoes.

Nutrition information per serving without using salt: calories, 89; fat, 2 grams; carbohydrate, 16 grams; cholesterol, 0 milligrams; sodium, 3 milligrams.

■ Butter-flavored granules add a delicious buttery flavor without loading these mashed potatoes with unnecessary fat and calories.

Garlic and Tarragon Mashed Potatoes

4 large potatoes, peeled
⅓ cup evaporated skim milk, heated
¼ teaspoon salt
¼ teaspoon white pepper
2 cloves garlic, minced
1 tablespoon dried tarragon
1 tablespoon diet margarine or 1 teaspoon imitation butter-flavored granules

Pierce potatoes with a fork. Place in a microwave-safe baking dish and cover. Microwave on high for 8 minutes. Allow potatoes to stand for 3 minutes. Using 2 knives, cut potatoes into pieces. Place potatoes in bowl of an electric mixer. Beat on low, adding warm evaporated skim milk by drops.

Gradually increase beater speed and add salt, white pepper, minced garlic, dried tarragon and diet margarine or butter-flavored granules. Spoon potatoes in mounds around a platter.

Makes 4 to 6 servings.

Nutrition information per serving: calories, 167; fat, 1.1 grams; carbohydrate, 34.6 grams; cholesterol, 1 milligram; sodium, 145 milligrams.

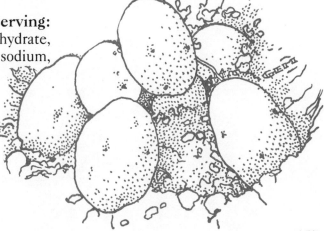

No Southern cook should be without a recipe for grits. This one is low in fat but has a terrific flavor and a delightful texture.

Grits and Cheese Souffle

2 tablespoons olive oil
1 tablespoon flour
2½ cups water
½ teaspoon salt
½ cup grits (not instant)
1 egg yolk
⅛ teaspoon cayenne pepper
¼ teaspoon thyme
1 cup (about 4 ounces) low-fat
  Cheddar cheese
3 egg whites
½ teaspoon cream of tartar
3 tablespoons Parmesan cheese
Non-stick cooking spray

Preheat oven to 375 F.

Heat the olive oil over medium heat in a large skillet. Whisk in the flour and cook 2 to 3 minutes, until flour begins to look golden brown.

Whisk in water, salt and grits. Stir constantly until mixture comes to a boil. Simmer, stirring occasionally, until mixture is thick and smooth, about 5 minutes. Remove from heat and allow to cool slightly.

In a small bowl, combine the egg yolk, cayenne pepper and thyme. Stir a small amount of the grits mixture into the egg mixture. Then stir the egg mixture back into the grits. (This is done to slowly warm up the egg mixture so that the heated grits mixture doesn't immediately cook the eggs when they are combined.) Add the Cheddar cheese and combine thoroughly.

In a large bowl, beat the egg whites and cream of tartar with an electric mixer until soft peaks form. Continue beating until egg whites are stiff and don't slide when the bowl is inverted.

Coat a 1-quart souffle dish or casserole with non-stick cooking spray. Gently fold the egg whites, ⅓ at a time, into the grits and cheese mixture. Pour the mixture in the prepared pan and sprinkle with grated parmesan cheese.

Bake in a hot oven until golden brown on top and firm in the center, about 35 to 40 minutes. Serve immediately.

Makes 8 servings.

Nutrition information per serving: calories, 135; fat, 8.7 grams; carbohydrate, 5 grams; cholesterol, 36 milligrams; sodium, 290 milligrams.

■ Greens are a new experience for many people, but they are incredibly delicious and packed with iron and other nutrients. Made this way, greens have virtually no fat.

New-Fashioned Greens

24 ounces collard greens and kale, mixed
½ pound lean smoked pork, trimmed of all visible fat
2 quarts water
2 slices of fresh lemon with peel (as for iced tea)
Salt to taste (optional)

Select fresh tender greens with no yellow leaves. Remove and discard the stems. Set aside.

Drop the trimmed ham and lemon slices into a large stainless steel or enamel kettle with 2 quarts water. Bring to a boil. Allow to boil, uncovered, for 30 minutes, until the water is reduced by half.

Wash the greens in at least 3 changes of water. They are usually very sandy, so wash carefully; drain.

Remove the ham and lemon slices from the pot. Discard the lemon and save the ham. Add the greens to the water in the kettle and reduce heat to a simmer. Simmer gently for 45 minutes, or until greens are tender.

Cut the reserved ham into slivers. Add ham to the greens and heat through. Taste for salt before serving; it may be unnecessary to add any. Drain the greens, if necessary, before serving.

Makes 6 servings.

Test kitchen notes: The flavor of greens improves if made in advance and allowed to mellow overnight. Reheat and serve with a small bottle of vinegar if desired.

Never use bacon fat or "drippings" to season greens. It clings to the leaves and makes the dish taste greasy. Serve greens with corn muffins, black-eyed peas and rice. Every variety of greens has a different flavor, so the cook may want to experiment.

Nutrition information per serving: calories, 130; fat, 5.4 grams; carbohydrate, 7.8 grams; cholesterol, 34 milligrams; sodium, 66 milligrams.

Kumquat Barbecue Sauce

1 cup low-sodium V-8 juice
½ cup dark brown sugar
½ teaspoon black pepper
½ teaspoon thyme
1 clove garlic chopped fine
¾ cup Kumquat Puree (recipe
   follows)

Add ingredients to large sauce pan. Bring to a boil and simmer uncovered for about 20 minutes or until the consistency of ketchup. Will thicken slightly as it cools.

Makes 1½ cups barbecue sauce.

Nutrition information per tablespoon: calories, 24; fat, 0 grams; carbohydrate, 5.9 grams; cholesterol, 0 milligrams; sodium, 4.7 milligrams.

Kumquat Puree

1 pound large ripe kumquats
1 cup water
5 tablespoons light corn syrup
¼ teaspoon ground ginger
½ cup white wine

To make kumquat puree, with small paring knife cut just through rind around middle of each kumquat. Pull apart and separate pulp from rind. Coarsely chop rinds and add to sauce pan with ½ cup water, 3 tablespoons light corn syrup and ¼ teaspoon ground ginger. Simmer covered for 45 minutes.

In a second sauce pan add pulp, ½ cup water and 2 tablespoons light corn syrup. Simmer covered for 45 minutes.

Let cool. Place pulp into strainer and with large spoon force pulp through strainer to remove seeds. Continue until only the heaviest pulp and seeds are left. Add rind, pulp and white wine to blender and puree.

Makes about 2 cups of puree.

Nutrition information per ¾ cup: calories, 264; fat, 0 grams; carbohydrate, 62.4 grams; cholesterol, 0 milligrams; sodium, 36 milligrams.

BREADS
and muffins

■ For an extra nutty flavor, toast the sunflower seeds before baking these muffins.

Sunflower Seed Bran Muffins

Cholesterol and saturated fat contribute to increased cholesterol levels in your body. However, cholesterol and saturated fat are not the same thing. Some foods can be low in cholesterol or contain no cholesterol and can still be high in saturated fat.

Foods high in saturated fat include vegetable shortening, snack foods and bakery goods made with tropical oils, hydrogenated peanut butter, solid margarine and chocolate.

Saturated fat is solid at room temperature. It is also found in marbled meats and whole-milk dairy products.

1 cup sunflower seeds
½ cup oat bran
½ cup cornmeal
1½ cups buttermilk
2 egg whites
2 tablespoons dark brown sugar
½ teaspoon thyme or oregano
3 tablespoons peanut oil
1½ cups unbleached flour
1 tablespoon baking powder
1 teaspoon soda
¼ teaspoon salt

Soak oat bran and cornmeal in buttermilk for 20 minutes.

Heat oven to 350 F and roast sunflower seeds until they are lightly browned; set aside.

Whisk together the egg whites, brown sugar, thyme or oregano and peanut oil. Stir until the sugar dissolves. Stir sugar and oil mixture into the buttermilk, oat bran and cornmeal mixture.

Stir flour, baking powder, soda and salt together well. Add the sunflower seeds to this mixture. Add the dry ingredients to the buttermilk mixture. Stir (not more than 10 seconds) to blend. Spoon into muffin tins, filling cups almost completely.

Bake at 400 F for 15 to 20 minutes.

Makes 12 muffins.

Nutrition information per serving: calories, 203; fat, 10.1 grams; carbohydrate, 22.2 grams; cholesterol, 1 milligram; sodium, 234 milligrams.

■ These airy, slate-blue muffins were made to be dunked.

New Mexico Blue Corn Muffins

1½ cups blue cornmeal
½ cup unbleached flour
3 teaspoons baking powder
1 teaspoon soda
¼ teaspoon salt
¼ teaspoon rubbed sage
¼ teaspoon cumin
2 eggs
1 tablespoon honey or sugar
1 tablespoon oil
1 cup buttermilk

Mix together blue cornmeal, flour, baking power, soda, salt and spices in a large bowl. In another bowl, whisk eggs with honey, oil and buttermilk. Make a well in the dry ingredients and quickly stir in the liquid, stirring not more than a few seconds. Batter will be thin. Spoon into greased muffin tins, filling tins at least ¾ full for rounded tops.

Bake at 400 F for 15 to 18 minutes or until muffins are lightly brown. Serve immediately with soups, Picadillo al Horno (page 83) or salads.

Makes 12 muffins.

Test kitchen notes: Blue corn, which is also called maiz azul, is from the Southwest. It is available in specialty and health-food stores or by mail-order. It has an attractive slate-blue color and distinctive flavor and aroma that remain after cooking.

Nutrition information per serving: calories, 113; fat, 2.8 grams; carbohydrate, 19.6 grams; cholesterol, 40 milligrams; sodium, 226 milligrams.

■ You might be tempted to serve these moist muffins just for breakfast but they are delicious for lunch, dinner and snacks as well.

Apple-Cinnamon Muffins

Tips for lighter baking

■ Use 2 egg whites in place of 1 whole egg in most quick breads, cookies and cakes.

■ Use low-fat or skim milk in place of whole milk.

■ Use 3 tablespoons of cocoa powder and 1 tablespoon canola oil for each ounce of baking chocolate.

■ Use 1 tablespoon of sugar per cup of flour for muffins, quick breads and biscuits.

■ Use no more than 2 tablespoons of fat per cup of flour for muffins, quick breads and biscuits.

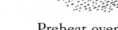

2¼ cups oat bran

1¼ teaspoons ground cinnamon

1 tablespoon baking powder

½ cup evaporated skim milk

¾ cup frozen apple juice
   concentrate

2 egg whites

2 tablespoons light corn syrup

1 medium apple, cored and
   chopped but not peeled

¼ cup chopped walnuts

Preheat oven to 425 F.

Mix the dry ingredients in a bowl. In a large bowl, mix the evaporated milk, juice concentrate, egg whites and corn syrup. Blend in the dry ingredients. Add the chopped apple and nuts. Line a muffin tin with paper muffin cups and fill with batter. Oat bran rises very little, so you can put more batter in each cup than you would if you were using wheat flour. Bake for 17 minutes.

Makes 15 muffins.

Test kitchen notes: These moist, slightly sweet muffins are great in a kid's lunch box. Bake ahead to allow the flavors to meld.

Nutrition information per serving: calories, 115; fat, 3.2 grams; carbohydrate, 17.2 grams; cholesterol, 0 milligrams; sodium, 100 milligrams.

■ This corn bread is a variation on traditional Southern versions. It is moist but not too sweet. A cast-iron skillet gives the cornbread a golden crust.

Corn bread

½ cup flour

1 tablespoon double-acting baking powder

½ teaspoon baking soda

½ teaspoon sugar (optional)

½ teaspoon salt

2 egg whites

1¼ cups stone-ground yellow cornmeal

2 tablespoons peanut oil

1¼ cups buttermilk

1 cup canned or frozen corn, drained

Preheat oven to 425 F. Coat a baking dish or a cast-iron skillet with non-stick cooking spray; set aside.

Mix flour, baking powder, soda, sugar, salt and cornmeal in a bowl.

In a separate dish, combine egg whites, oil and buttermilk. Stir well to combine. Stir buttermilk mixture into cornmeal mixture in about 10 strokes. Do not overbeat. Stir in corn. Pour into prepared pan. Bake 25 to 30 minutes. Serve hot with a sugarless fruit spread or jam.

Makes 6 servings.

Nutrition information per serving: calories, 233; fat, 5.1 grams; carbohydrate, 39.9 grams; cholesterol, 2 milligrams; sodium, 417 milligrams.

■ Olive oil gives this garlic bread a delicious flavor and fragrance.

Garlic Bread

4 large slices French or Italian
   bread
4 tablespoons olive oil
1 clove garlic, crushed
½ teaspoon tarragon, basil or
   salad herbs, crumbled
4 tablespoons grated Parmesan
   cheese

Put bread on a baking sheet. In a food processor or blender, combine oil and garlic. Process until garlic is pureed. Drizzle mixture over bread. Sprinkle herbs and cheese over bread. Broil until bread toasts.
Makes 4 servings.

Nutrition information per serving: calories, 226; fat, 15.3 grams; carbohydrate, 17.4 grams; cholesterol, 4 milligrams; sodium, 269 milligrams.

■ Herbs, olive oil and high-fiber whole-wheat flour make these low-fat breadsticks delicious. Prepare a batch ahead and freeze for later.

Whole-Wheat Bread Sticks or Pizza Dough

1¼ cups whole-wheat flour

¾ cup warm water

1 package dry active yeast

¼ teaspoon sugar

¾ cup unbleached flour or bread flour

2 tablespoons olive oil

½ teaspoon salt

Non-stick cooking spray, preferably with olive oil

1 tablespoon dried herbs, such as basil, oregano or rosemary

1 teaspoon sesame seeds

In a large bowl, combine ¼ cup of the whole-wheat flour with ¼ cup of the warm water, yeast and sugar. Allow to stand undisturbed for 30 minutes. It should become foamy and fragrant.

Stir in the remaining water, flours, 1 tablespoon of olive oil and salt. Stir until mixture forms a sticky dough, then turn out on a board and knead. Sprinkle board lightly with additional flour if necessary to prevent sticking. Knead until dough becomes smooth and elastic, about 10 minutes.

Shape dough into a ball. Spray bowl and dough lightly with non-stick spray. Cover with wax paper and allow to rise 45 minutes to 1 hour, until puffy and almost doubled in bulk.

Punch down dough and divide in half. Freeze other half for another use. Divide remaining half into 4 pieces. Roll each piece into a rope about 10 inches long. Twist and pinch edges. Place on a baking sheet, brush with remaining 1 tablespoon olive oil and sprinkle with herbs and sesame seeds.

Allow to rise 30 minutes, until puffy.

Preheat oven to 400 F.

Bake bread sticks for 15 to 20 minutes, until golden brown and lightly crusty. Serve hot.

Makes 8 servings.

Nutrition information per serving: calories, 135; fat, 4.1 grams; carbohydrate, 21.1 grams; cholesterol, 0 milligrams; sodium, 147 milligrams.

How to knead dough

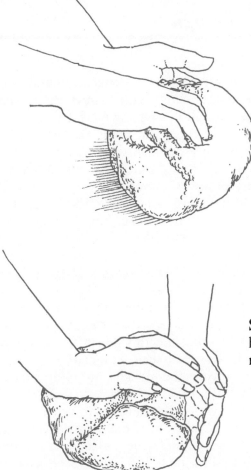

Step 1: Shape the dough into a ball and, on a lightly floured surface, fold it toward you.

Step 2: Using the heels of your hands, push the dough with a rolling motion and give it a quarter turn.

Step 3: Continue kneading for 8 to 10 minutes until dough is smooth and elastic and doesn't stick.

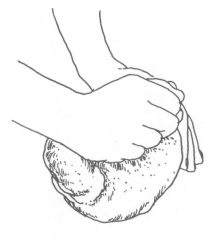

e-wheat flour produces a more tender, flaky crust than white flour. The wheat in the flour also lends a slightly nutty flavor.

Whole-Wheat Herbed Pizza Dough

1 cup plus 2 tablespoons flour
½ cup whole wheat flour
1 package active dry yeast
½ teaspoon thyme
½ teaspoon salt
½ cup warm water (120 F)
1 tablespoon olive oil

To prepare pizza dough, combine white flour and ½ cup whole wheat flour, yeast, thyme and salt in a mixing bowl.

Add ½ cup warm water (120 F) and 1 tablespoon olive oil; beat with electric mixer until smooth. Knead until smooth and elastic. Cover; let rise 30 minutes.

Shape pizza dough into 12-inch circle on an ungreased pizza stone. Sprinkle dough with desired ingredients. Bake at 450 F for 15 to 20 minutes.

Makes 1 (12-inch) pizza or enough for 4 people.

Test kitchen notes: This recipe makes a drier, crustier dough than the recipe on page 168. If desired, use this dough to make focaccia, which is an Italian flatbread. To make focaccia, divide the dough into 4 rounds and lightly brush each with 1 teaspoon of olive oil. Sprinkle with salt and freshly ground black pepper and allow to rise 1 hour longer. Using your fingers, dimple the surface of each focaccia. Bake in a preheated 400 F oven until surfaces are lightly brown, about 25 minutes. Remove from oven and allow to cool, flipping occasionally so steam doesn't cause the dough to become soggy.

Serve warm with Greek Hummus (page 7), Red-Hot Dip (page 5) or Tapenade Spread (page 3).

Nutrition information per serving: calories, 202; fat, 3.8 grams; carbohydrate, 35.9 grams; cholesterol, 0 milligrams; sodium, 294 milligrams.

■ A mix of flours, vegetables and herbs gives this easy, no-knead bread a deep, zesty flavor. Serve it toasted, too.

Vegetable Batter Bread

2 cups all-purpose flour or 1 cup all-purpose and 1 cup bread flour
1 cup whole-wheat flour
½ cup wheat germ
1 package dry-active yeast
½ teaspoon salt or salt substitute
1¼ cups water
2 tablespoons olive oil
1 tablespoon honey or brown sugar
1 egg
1 cup carrot, grated
1 medium onion, finely chopped
¼ cup fresh parsley or basil, chopped
½ teaspoon poppy seeds
½ teaspoon freshly ground black pepper
½ teaspoon dried tarragon, crushed
1 clove garlic, crushed through a press
Non-stick cooking spray

In the bowl of a mixer or food processor, combine the flour or bread flour, whole-wheat flour, wheat germ, yeast and salt or salt substitute. Stir to blend all ingredients.

In a microwave-safe bowl or a saucepan, bring the water, olive oil and honey or brown sugar to a simmer. Allow to cool to 120 F or until it is warm to the touch. Add water and egg to the flours and yeast in the food processor work bowl. Process well.

Add the carrot, onion, parsley, poppy seeds, black pepper, tarragon and garlic to the flour mixture. Process well to mix. (About 1 minute in a food processor; 3 minutes on medium speed in a mixer.) Mixture should pull away from sides of bowl.

Spray a 2-quart souffle dish, baking pan or oval casserole dish with non-stick cooking spray. Spoon mixture into prepared dish and cover lightly with plastic wrap. Set aside in a warm place and let rise until double in size and rounded on top.

Bake in a preheated 350 F oven until golden brown on top and top sounds hollow when thumped lightly.

Cool for 15 minutes. Remove from baking dish and cool for 10 minutes longer. Serve warm.

Makes 12 servings.

Nutrition information per serving: calories, 176; fat, 3.7 grams; carbohydrate, 30.6 grams; cholesterol, 23 milligrams; sodium, 107 milligrams.

DESSERTS

■ Mango trees were imported to Florida after the Civil War and now flourish in South Florida's subtropical climate. From June to September, there is abundant fresh, sweet fruit to use in mousse.

Postre de Mango

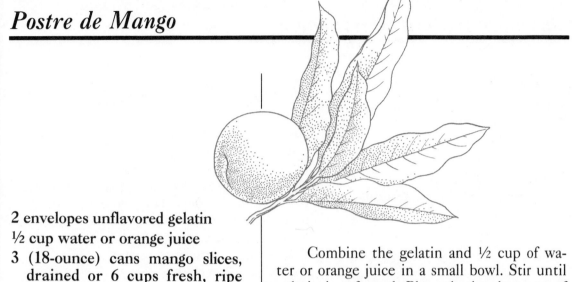

2 envelopes unflavored gelatin

½ cup water or orange juice

3 (18-ounce) cans mango slices, drained or 6 cups fresh, ripe mango

2 (14-ounce) cans sweetened condensed milk

⅓ cup dark rum

2 teaspoons vanilla extract

½ cup lime juice

2 pints strawberries, rinsed and stems removed (reserve a few whole berries for garnish)

Combine the gelatin and ½ cup of water or orange juice in a small bowl. Stir until gelatin is softened. Place the bowl on top of a small saucepan of simmering water. Saucepan should just cradle bowl so that heat of the simmering water warms the underside of the bowl. When gelatin dissolves, set aside.

Combine mangoes, condensed milk, rum, vanilla and lime juice in the bowl of a food processor or blender. Puree mixture until smooth. Add gelatin and puree again. Pour into a mold and lay a sheet of plastic wrap directly over the surface. Refrigerate at least 5 hours before serving. This dessert can be prepared several days in advance if tightly covered.

Puree the hulled strawberries in a blender or food processor. Unmold the mango mousse onto a serving platter. Pour the pureed strawberries around the mousse and garnish with whole berries.

Makes 14 servings.

Nutrition information per serving: calories, 258; fat, 5.2 grams; carbohydrate, 46.9 grams; cholesterol, 19 milligrams; sodium, 74 milligrams.

173

■ For the crunchiest, nuttiest meringues, make them on a day without rain in the forecast. In humid weather, meringues become damp and sticky.

Chocolate Walnut Meringues

4 egg whites

1 teaspoon vanilla extract

⅛ teaspoon cream of tartar

½ cup sugar

2 tablespoons unsweetened cocoa powder

1 cup toasted walnuts, ground

Preheat the oven to 225 F.

Beat egg whites until foamy. Add vanilla and cream of tartar and continue to beat, adding sugar and cocoa 1 teaspoon at a time, until stiff peaks form. Fold in walnuts. Drop mixture by rounded teaspoons on a cookie sheet lined with parchment paper. Bake meringues for 1 hour. Turn heat off and let cookies rest in oven for 5 minutes. Remove and let cool in a dry place. Store baked meringues in an airtight container.

Makes 36 cookies.

Nutrition information per cookie: calories, 27; fat, 1.3 grams; carbohydrate, 3.3 grams; cholesterol, 0 milligrams; sodium, 6 milligrams.

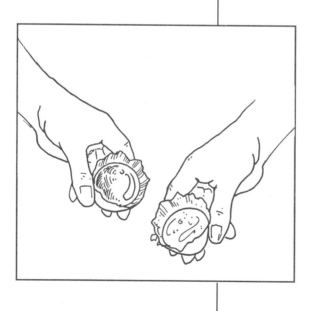

Step 1: Separate the eggs while they are cold. However, let the egg whites come to room temperature before starting.

Step 2: Use glass, stainless steel or copper bowls for whipping egg whites. The bowl and the beaters should be freshly cleaned and completely dry.

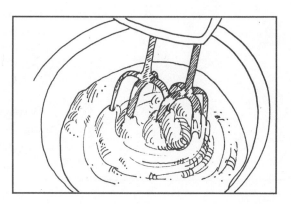

Step 3: Egg whites beaten to soft peaks have soft tips that curl over when the beaters are lifted.

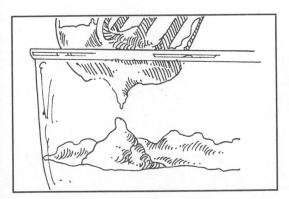

Step 4: Egg whites beaten to stiff peaks will stand straight when the beater are lifted.

■ This easy pie is delicious eaten right away but it can also be frozen and enjoyed later. If you prefer, substitute raspberries for blueberries.

Blueberry Lemon Pie

1 package (4-serving size) lemon-flavored gelatin
⅔ cup boiling water
½ cup cold water
Ice cubes
3½ cups thawed whipped topping
1 pint fresh blueberries
Prepared 9-inch graham cracker crust

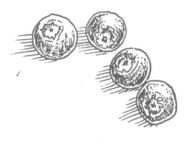

Completely dissolve gelatin in boiling water. Combine water and ice cubes to make 1½ cups. Add to gelatin, stirring until slightly thickened. Remove any unmelted ice.

Using a wire whisk, blend in the whipped topping. Fold in 1½ cups fresh blueberries and chill until mixture will mound. It may appear that you have too much filling but this mixture mounds nicely and makes an attractive high pie. Spoon all of the chilled mixture into pie crust. Chill pie overnight.

Garnish with remaining blueberries and additional whipped topping before serving.

Makes 1 (9-inch) pie.

Test kitchen notes: Frozen blueberries cannot be substituted for fresh in this recipe.

Nutrition information per serving: calories, 241; fat, 14.6 grams; carbohydrate, 26.2 grams; cholesterol, 0 milligrams; sodium, 198 milligrams.

Blueberry fast facts

■ Florida harvests the earliest blueberries of the season, beginning in May.

■ Florida ranks 28th in terms of production. Michigan ranks first.

■ Blueberries are a good source of vitamins A and C, as well as potassium, phosphorus, calcium and fiber.

■ Blueberries contain only 62 calories in 100 grams, less than a gram of fat and almost no sodium.

■ The pastel pink color and the cloudlike texture of the watermelon filling make this a cooling dessert for a hot summer day.

Watermelon Chiffon Pie

About 3½ pounds ripe
  watermelon
⅓ cup sugar
⅛ teaspoon salt
2 envelopes unflavored gelatin
1 tablespoon lemon juice
Dash cream of tartar
2 egg whites
2 tablespoons sugar
½ cup whipping cream
1 (9-inch) graham cracker crust
Watermelon balls

Words on watermelon

■ Florida is the country's largest producer of watermelons, followed by Texas and Georgia. About 54,000 acres, worth about $70 million annually, are planted in Florida.

■ Americans eat about 13 pounds of watermelon per person per year.

■ Watermelon isn't a nutritional powerhouse for any one nutrient, but it's a good source of fiber and complex carbohydrates and is low in calories and sodium.

Here is what watermelon offers per 100 grams (3½ ounces):

Calories	26
Protein	0.5 gram
Fat	0.2 gram
Carbohydrates	6.4 grams
Calcium	7 milligrams
Iron	0.5 milligram
Sodium	1 milligram
Vitamin A	500 I.U. *
Vitamin C	7 milligrams

* Vitamin A is measured in international units.
SOURCE: USDA research

Cut off and discard melon rind. Cut fruit into cubes. Whirl melon cubes in a blender or food processor until smooth. Pour through a fine wire strainer set over a bowl; discard pulp and seeds. You should have 3 cups watermelon juice.

Pour melon juice into a saucepan and stir in 1/3 cup sugar and salt. Sprinkle gelatin over juice mixture and let stand for about 5 minutes to soften. Stir over medium heat until gelatin and sugar are completely dissolved, then stir in lemon juice.

Cover gelatin mixture and refrigerate until mixture is thick enough to mound slightly when dropped from a spoon (about 1 hour).

In large bowl of an electric mixer, beat cream of tartar and egg whites until they hold stiff peaks. Sprinkle 2 tablespoons of sugar over whites and continue beating until glossy. Fold whites into melon mixture.

In small bowl of mixer, beat cream until it holds stiff peaks; fold into melon mixture. Spoon into crust.

Cover pie lightly and refrigerate until filling is firm (at least 6 hours). Garnish with watermelon balls before serving.

Makes 8 servings.

Test kitchen notes: The riper the watermelon, the sweeter the pie will be. Taste the watermelon mixture before adding the gelatin. If it isn't sweet enough, increase the 1/3 cup sugar to 1/2 cup.

Nutrition information per serving: calories, 257; fat, 13.5 grams; carbohydrate, 32.3 grams; cholesterol, 20 milligrams; sodium, 188 milligrams.

■ If you love cheesecake, you will really enjoy this slimmed-down tropical version.

Low-Fat Pineapple Cheese Pie

Crust:

5 whole graham crackers, crushed

¼ cup almonds, ground to a paste

1 tablespoon low-fat yogurt

Filling:

¼ cup water

3 tablespoons sugar

1 envelope unflavored gelatin

1 cup unsweetened pineapple juice

3 cups low-fat cottage cheese

3 tablespoons sugar

1 (8½-ounce) can crushed pineapple, packed in its own juice

3 teaspoons cornstarch

1 tablespoon water

1 teaspoon orange liqueur

Combine graham cracker crumbs, almonds and yogurt. Spray an 8-inch pie plate with non-stick coating. Press crust up sides and bottom of pan; refrigerate.

In a blender or food processor, combine water, 3 tablespoons sugar and gelatin. Allow to stand for 5 minutes to soften gelatin. In a separate pan, bring pineapple juice to a boil. Pour over gelatin mixture and blend for 30 seconds to mix; cool. Add cottage cheese and 3 tablespoons sugar to blender or food processor. Blend until smooth and creamy. Pour into prepared crust. Chill several hours or overnight.

About 2 hours before serving, combine crushed pineapple, cornstarch and water. Bring to a boil, stirring frequently, until thickened. Remove from heat. Stir in orange liqueur. Cool to room temperature and spread over pie.

Chill pineapple-mixture-topped pie 2 hours before serving.

Makes 12 servings.

Nutrition information per serving: calories, 170; fat, 4.1 grams; carbohydrate, 24.3 grams; cholesterol, 5 milligrams; sodium, 335 milligrams.

■ With a microwave oven, you can quickly make these crunchy, after-school cookies with your children or grandchildren.

Honey-Peanut Butter Granola Bars

⅔ cup honey
¾ cup chunky peanut butter
4 cups granola mix

In a 4-cup microwave-safe container cook honey on high (100 percent) power in microwave oven for 2 to 3 minutes or until honey boils. Stir in peanut butter; mix until thoroughly blended. Place granola in large bowl. Pour honey mixture over granola and combine thoroughly. Press firmly into 13-by-9-by-2-inch baking pan. Let stand until firm. Cut into bars.

Makes 36 bars.

Test kitchen notes: Read the package labels to determine if the granola mix contains coconut, coconut or palm oil. Tropical oils are loaded with saturated fat and should be avoided. Substitute another high-fiber cereal instead, if needed.

Nutrition information per serving: calories, 106; fat, 4.9 grams; carbohydrate, 14.7 grams; cholesterol, 0 milligrams; sodium, 52 milligrams.

Healthy snacks for children

■ Low-fat milk, cheeses and ice milk.
■ Fruit smoothies.
■ Crunchy breakfast cereals that are low in fat and sodium eaten dry.
■ Raisins, dried apricots, dried cherries.
■ Fresh fruit and berries.
■ Unsalted pretzels.
■ Peanut butter in celery sticks.
■ Hot-air popped popcorn.
■ Angel-food cake.
■ Gingersnaps or devil's food cake cookies.

■ If your children enjoy making their own snacks, they will love these healthy, fruit-packed cookies.

Crunchy Peanut Butter Clusters

2 cups whole cashews, almonds or walnut halves

½ cup wheat germ

6 ounces golden raisins

3 ounces dried apricots, chopped

½ cup oats (quick or old-fashioned, uncooked)

¼ cup firmly packed brown sugar

⅔ cup light corn syrup

¼ cup peanut butter

Heat oven to 350 F.

Combine cashews, wheat germ, raisins, apricots and oats.

In a small, heavy saucepan, combine remaining ingredients. Bring mixture to a boil over medium heat, stirring constantly. Immediately pour over nut mixture, stirring until well-coated. Drop mixture by rounded tablespoonfuls onto a greased cookie sheet.

Bake 8 to 10 minutes or until golden brown. Cool 5 minutes on a cookie sheet; remove to wire rack and cool. Store loosely covered.

Makes 2 dozen clusters.

Test kitchen notes: These cookies freeze well. When ready to eat, let thaw in the refrigerator or warm in microwave on medium-high (80 percent) power for 1 minute.

Nutrition information per serving: calories, 156; fat, 7.1 grams; carbohydrate, 22.2 grams; cholesterol, 0 milligrams; sodium, 25 milligrams.

These cookies are soft and moist eaten hot from the oven. Once cooled, they become crisp and crunchy.

Oatmeal Cookies

¾ cup light corn syrup
¼ cup water
1 teaspoon vanilla extract
2 egg whites
½ teaspoon cinnamon
1 cup brown sugar
½ cup granulated sugar
2 cups rolled oats
2 cups oat bran
1 cup all-purpose flour
½ teaspoon baking soda
Raisins, currants, chopped nuts
  or dates (optional)

Preheat oven to 350 F.

Mix all the moist ingredients and sugars in a large bowl, then gradually blend in dry ingredients. Drop teaspoonfuls onto a cookie sheet lightly sprayed with non-stick coating. Bake 15 to 17 minutes or until edges are browned. (The larger the cookie, the longer the baking time.)

Makes about 2 dozen cookies.

Nutrition information per serving: calories, 145; fat, 1.2 grams; carbohydrate, 30.6 grams; cholesterol, 0 milligrams; sodium, 31 milligrams.

■ Experiment with your favorite toppings for this rich, brownielike cake. It is so chocolaty, you could eat it plain.

Chocolate Citrus Cake

2 cups cake flour
1½ cups sugar
½ cup cocoa powder
1 tablespoon instant coffee
2 teaspoons baking soda
⅔ cup peanut oil
½ cup buttermilk
Mandarin orange sections
½ teaspoon vanilla
3 egg whites, at room
  temperature
Citrus filling:
3 tablespoons water
½ cup non-fat yogurt, drained
1 tablespoon orange peel,
  grated
8 ounces part skim ricotta
  cheese
¼ cup confectioners' sugar
1 tablespoon orange
  marmalade
1 tablespoon orange liqueur
1 tablespoon unflavored
  gelatin

Preheat oven to 350 F.

Coat a 9-inch cake pan with non-stick spray. Sift together cake flour, sugar, cocoa, instant coffee and baking soda. Combine the oil, buttermilk and vanilla. Beat egg whites until stiff but not dry. Stir liquids into flour mixture to make a soupy batter.

Fold egg whites into batter by thirds; do not stir. Pour batter into pan. Bake for 30 minutes or until cake is firm on sides. Cake will fall in center, giving it a brownielike texture. Combine filling ingredients except gelatin and water. Dissolve gelatin on top of 3 tablespoons of water. Melt gelatin mixture in microwave on medium (50 percent power) until syrupy, about 30 seconds. Stir into filling mixture. Chill. Spread filling on top of cake, making the center even with sides. Garnish with orange sections.

Makes 10 servings.

Nutrition information per serving: calories, 435; fat, 17.3 grams; carbohydrate, 63.4 grams; cholesterol, 7 milligrams; sodium, 231 milligrams.

Some good news for chocoholics

■ Substitute 2 tablespoons of cocoa powder, plus 1 tablespoon of oil for 1 square of baking chocolate in most recipes.

■ Use ½ cup cocoa powder plus ⅔ cup corn syrup to make fat-free chocolate syrup.

■ Use 2 tablespoons homemade, fat-free chocolate syrup, 1 cup skim milk and ½ cup ice milk to make a low-fat chocolate milkshake.

■ Use ½ cup warm, fat-free homemade chocolate syrup, 1 firm banana and ½ pint fresh strawberries to make chocolate fondue for two.

■ Use 3 tablespoons of cocoa powder mixed with 2 tablespoons of commercial sugarless fruit spread to make a chocolate icing.

■ Everybody loves ice cream — especially during summer in Florida. Fruit and low-fat yogurt make this version easy on your diet.

Peach 'Ice Cream'

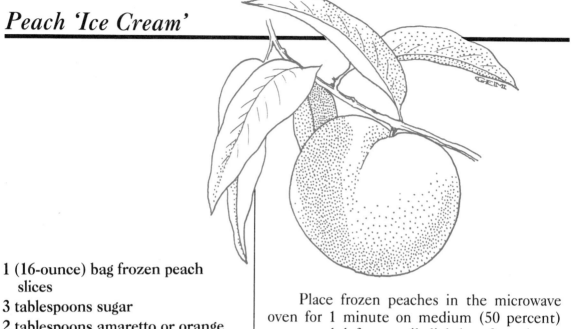

1 (16-ounce) bag frozen peach
   slices
3 tablespoons sugar
2 tablespoons amaretto or orange
   flavored liqueur
¼ teaspoon almond extract
¼ cup low-fat vanilla yogurt

Place frozen peaches in the microwave oven for 1 minute on medium (50 percent) power and defrost until slightly softened.

Combine the peaches, sugar, amaretto liqueur and yogurt in a food processor. Process until smooth and icy. Serve immediately or freeze for 30 minutes.

If freezing for longer, break peach ice cream into pieces and process again in the food processor to obtain a smooth, creamy consistency.

Makes 4 servings.

Test kitchen notes: For faster results, place the food processor blade and bowl in the freezer for 30 minutes before starting recipe. If you need to increase the amount of servings, prepare the recipe in separate batches rather than doubling ingredients.

Nutrition information per serving: calories, 181; fat, 0.5 grams; carbohydrate, 39.8 grams; cholesterol, 1 milligram; sodium, 26 milligrams.

■ From January until May, try this low-fat recipe with fresh Florida strawberries.

Strawberry 'Ice Cream'

1 (16-ounce) bag frozen,
   unsweetened strawberries

2 tablespoons sugar

¼ cup low-fat plain yogurt

2 tablespoons frozen, concentrated
   lemonade

Mint sprigs for garnish

Place bag of strawberries in microwave oven and cook on medium power (50 percent) until partially defrosted.

Combine the berries, sugar, yogurt and lemonade in a food processor and blend until smooth and icy. Serve immediately or freeze for 30 minutes longer. If freezing longer than 30 minutes, process again to obtain a smooth, icy consistency.

Makes 4 servings.

Test kitchen notes: If desired, use fresh, stemmed strawberries for this recipe. Make sure they are very ripe. The riper the fruit, the tastier the ice cream.

For faster results, place the food processor blade and bowl in the freezer for 30 minutes before starting recipe. If you need to increase the amount of servings, prepare the recipe in separate batches rather than doubling ingredients.

Nutrition information per serving: calories, 88; fat, 0.2 grams; carbohydrate, 20.7 grams; cholesterol, 1 milligram; sodium, 24 milligrams.

You may find it hard to believe this rich dessert is so low in fat and calories. Try it with other tropical fruits such as mango, pineapple or papaya.

Fresh Melon Sorbet

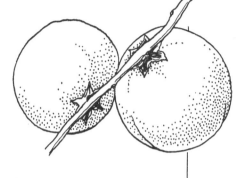

Other fruits to use to make sorbet

■ Citrus fruits, such as oranges, lemons, limes and tangerines.

■ Tart fruits such as persimmons and pineapples.

■ Tropical fruits, such as papayas, mangoes, kiwis and carambolas.

■ Berries such as raspberries, blackberries or blueberries. (Strain seeds and skins before freezing).

■ Tree fruits, such as apricots, cherries or plums.

■ Grapes, such as Red Flame, champagne or Concord. (Strain out skins and seeds before freezing.)

■ Watermelons and cantaloupes.

1 very ripe honeydew melon, peeled and chopped
1½ tablespoons sugar
Pinch nutmeg
1 tablespoon melon liqueur or orange liqueur

Combine the fruit, sugar and nutmeg in the bowl of a food processor. Puree until smooth and silky. Pour into a metal bowl or cake pan and freeze for 45 minutes to 1 hour, or until solid.

Break frozen puree into chunks and return to processor; add melon or orange liqueur. Process until icy and smooth. Serve immediately or freeze for another 30 minutes before serving.

Makes 4 servings.

Test kitchen notes: For faster results, place the food processor blade and bowl in the freezer for 30 minutes before starting recipe. The riper the honeydew melon, the tastier the sorbet. If you need to increase the amount of servings, prepare the recipe in separate batches rather than doubling ingredients.

Nutrition information per serving: calories, 142; fat, 0.3 grams; carbohydrate, 35.3 grams; cholesterol, 0 milligrams; sodium, 32 milligrams.

■ Rich textures and great flavors make this cheesecake unbeatable, yet it is surprisingly low in calories and fat.

Orange Cheesecake With Raspberry Sauce

1⅓ cups crunchy, nutlike cereal nuggets

1 tablespoon sugar

½ teaspoon cinnamon

2 tablespoons corn-oil margarine, melted

1 whole egg

2 egg whites

3 tablespoons orange juice

1½ teaspoons vanilla extract

⅓ cup sugar

2 teaspoons freshly grated orange zest (peel) or dried orange peel

1½ pounds (3 cups) 1-percent milk fat cottage cheese

1 (8-ounce) container low-fat vanilla yogurt

Raspberry Sauce (recipe follows)

Preheat oven to 375 F.

In a mixing bowl, combine cereal nuggets, 1 tablespoon sugar, cinnamon and melted margarine. Mix well to coat cereal. Press onto the bottom and sides of a 10-inch springform pan. Bake for 10 minutes. Remove from oven and cool while preparing filling.

Reduce oven temperature to 325 F.

In a blender, mixing bowl or food processor, combine the whole egg, egg whites, orange juice and peel, vanilla, cottage cheese and sugar. Blend until smooth. Pour into crust.

Bake slowly until the center of the cake is set, about 40 minutes. Remove from oven and spoon yogurt over top, spreading to edge of crust. Bake 15 minutes longer. Remove from oven and allow to cool to room temperature. Refrigerate at least 2 hours before serving.

Spoon Raspberry Sauce over individual servings of cheesecake.

Makes 10 servings.

Nutrition information per serving without raspberry sauce: calories, 198; fat, 4.3 grams; carbohydrate, 26.7 grams; cholesterol, 24 milligrams; sodium, 437 milligrams.

■ Serve this brilliantly colored sauce with almost any dessert.

Raspberry Sauce

1 (12-ounce) package frozen raspberries, thawed with juice
2 tablespoons powdered sugar (packed) or granulated sugar
1 teaspoon lemon or lime juice
½ teaspoon vanilla extract

Combine raspberries, powdered sugar or granulated sugar, lime or lemon juice and vanilla extract in the bowl of a food processor or blender. Puree mixture. Pour sauce through a strainer, pressing to separate juice from seeds; discard seeds.

Serve sauce warm or cold. Can be refrigerated for up to a week or frozen for 3 months. This is an excellent all-purpose dessert sauce that can be served over Peach Ice Cream (page 184), Fresh Melon Sorbet (page 186), fresh fruit or a slice of pound cake.

Makes 1 cup.

Nutrition information per serving: calories, 41; fat, 0.1 gram; carbohydrate, 10.4 grams; cholesterol, 0 milligrams; sodium, 0 milligrams.

Use these fruits to make delicious dessert sauces:
Blueberries
Blackberries
Strawberries
Fresh or dried apricots
Cranberries
Pineapples
Papayas
Pomegranates
Mangoes

188

■ Once you try this no-yolk version of carrot cake, you may never crave high-fat, high-cholesterol cakes again.

Oat Bran Carrot Cake With Cream Cheese Frosting

2 cups oat bran hot cereal
1 cup brown sugar
1 teaspoon baking powder
1 teaspoon baking soda
1 teaspoon salt
1 teaspoon ground cinnamon
1 cup apple juice
3 cups carrots, shredded
½ cup peanut oil
4 large egg whites
Cream cheese frosting:
8 ounces reduced fat cream cheese
2 tablespoons corn syrup
1 teaspoon vanilla
1 cup powdered sugar

Preheat oven to 350 F.

Coat a 13-by-9-inch baking pan thoroughly with non-stick cooking spray.

In a mixing bowl or food processor, combine oat bran cereal, brown sugar, baking powder, baking soda, salt and cinnamon. Mix and add apple juice, carrots, oil and egg whites. Beat only until ingredients are combined.

Pour into prepared pan. Bake until firm to the touch, about 40 minutes. Remove from oven and cool completely. Remove cake from pan.

In a mixing bowl or food processor, combine cream cheese, corn syrup and vanilla. Beat until smooth. Gradually beat in powdered sugar until fluffy. Spread icing on top of cooled cake.

Makes 15 servings.

Nutrition information per serving: calories, 285; fat, 13 grams; carbohydrate, 36 grams; cholesterol, 15 milligrams; sodium, 310 milligrams.

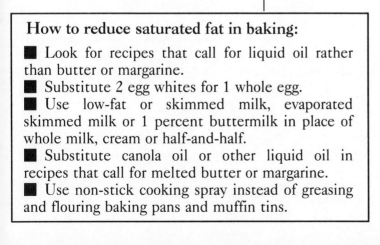

How to reduce saturated fat in baking:

■ Look for recipes that call for liquid oil rather than butter or margarine.
■ Substitute 2 egg whites for 1 whole egg.
■ Use low-fat or skimmed milk, evaporated skimmed milk or 1 percent buttermilk in place of whole milk, cream or half-and-half.
■ Substitute canola oil or other liquid oil in recipes that call for melted butter or margarine.
■ Use non-stick cooking spray instead of greasing and flouring baking pans and muffin tins.

■ Frozen puff pastry — available in the freezer section of most grocery stores — makes this attractive dessert easy to create at home.

Glazed Fruit Pizza

1 cup ricotta cheese

⅓ cup sugar

¼ teaspoon vanilla

1 sheet frozen puff pastry (½ of a 17-ounce package), thawed

3 cups thinly sliced seasonal fruit, such as pears, peaches, apples, strawberries or grapes

⅓ cup apricot preserves

Preheat oven to 425 F.

Whip together ricotta, sugar and vanilla; set aside.

On a lightly floured board, roll out puff pastry as thinly as possible. Cut a 16-inch circle. Roll up an inch along the edge of dough to form a lip. If desired, crimp with the tines of a fork for decoration.

Place crust in a pizza pan or in a tart pan with a removable bottom. Chill for 15 minutes or while slicing fruit. Spread chilled crust with ricotta mixture. Arrange fruit in a decorative pattern over filling. Bake for 25 minutes. For the last 5 minutes, turn oven to broil and lightly brown edges of the fruit. Remove from heat.

Strain apricot preserves into a saucepan or microwave-safe djsh. Melt preserves and brush over top of fruit to make a glaze.

Serve warm.

Makes 10 servings.

Nutrition information per serving: calories, 210; fat, 10.5 grams; carbohydrate, 25.9 grams; cholesterol, 8 milligrams; sodium, 31 milligrams.

■ Other parts of the United States are finally getting a taste of one of Florida's most exotic fruits — sweet-tart carambolas or star fruits.

Carambola Chiffon Pie in Graham Cracker Crust

Crust:

15 whole graham crackers

¼ cup powdered sugar

4 tablespoons low-calorie, whipped margarine, melted

2 tablespoons rum

Filling:

5 ripe carambolas

½ cup sugar

1 envelope unflavored gelatin

¼ cup low-fat ricotta cheese

⅔ cup water

1 tablespoon lime juice

1 tablespoon rum

3 egg whites

¼ cup sugar

Grind whole graham crackers in a blender to make crumbs or process them in a food processor until fine. Add sugar and blend again. Add melted margarine and rum by droplets until the crumbs stick together. Pat crumb mixture into a pie plate; chill.

Peel four carambolas and remove the seeds. (Slice lengthwise and push out the seeds with the tip of a knife.) Puree carambolas in a blender or food processor, scraping down the sides of the bowl frequently; set aside.

In a saucepan combine ½ cup sugar, gelatin and ricotta cheese. Beat with a whisk until sugar has dissolved. Whisk in water. Place saucepan over medium-high heat and whisk until mixture comes to a boil. Remove from heat and stir in lime juice and rum.

Stir gelatin mixture into carambola puree.

Refrigerate until mixture begins to thicken.

Beat 3 egg whites until stiff. Add ¼ cup sugar by sprinkles until egg whites are glossy. Egg whites should not slide when the bowl is inverted.

Fold egg whites gently into thickened carambola mixture. Pour into pie shell and chill until set. Slice remaining carambola crosswise into thin stars. Arrange slices on top of pie. Serve cold.

Makes 8 servings.

Nutrition information per serving: calories, 381; fat, 9.8 grams; carbohydrate, 61.9 grams; cholesterol, 2 milligrams; sodium, 418.8 milligrams.

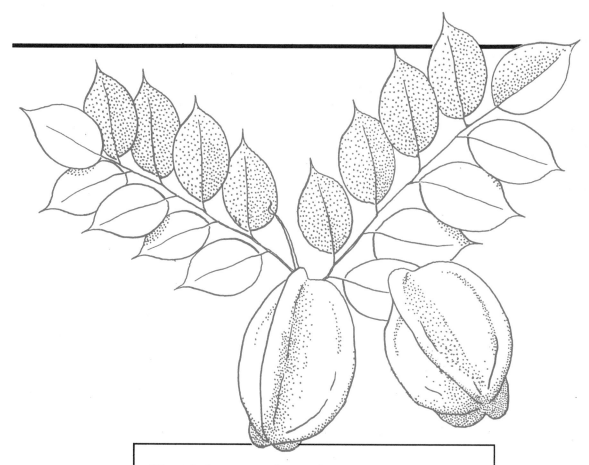

Florida's tropical starfruit

■ It is really a carambola but is called starfruit because of its star shape when the fruit is cut crosswise.

■ The flavor is both tart and sweet and the texture is crisp near the skin and soft in the center.

■ Ripe carambola can be eaten out of hand as a snack, sliced for desserts, sauteed and used as a garnish for meat or frozen to make ice creams or sorbets.

■ Look for shiny, firm, unblemished fruit.

■ If eating out of hand, you do not have to peel carambola. Wash the skin thoroughly and trim away brown edges. Discard the inedible seeds in the center.

■ One fruit yields about 1 cup of slices. One cup has about 80 calories.

■ Preserved this way, carambolas make terrific holiday gifts.

Brandied Carambola Slices

1 cup sugar
1 cup water
4 ripe carambolas
½ cup brandy or rum

Combine water and sugar in a heavy saucepan. Stir to dissolve sugar. Bring to a boil for 5 minutes, until mixture is syrupy. Allow to cool. Stir brandy or rum into syrup.

Wash and slice carambolas crosswise into stars. Remove the seeds, but reserve any juice. Push out the seeds with the tip of a knife. Add carambola slices to syrup.

Store in a clean jar with a tightfitting lid. Refrigerate until ready to serve. Serve over cereal or pound cake. Also good for garnish on baked ham, roast turkey or chicken.

Makes 2 pints.

Nutrition information per serving: calories, 73; fat, 0.1 gram; carbohydrate, 12.4 grams; cholesterol, 0 milligrams; sodium, 0.6 milligrams.

■ This easy angel food cake made with cocoa powder is devilishly good. Make sure your egg whites are room temperature before beginning.

Chocolate Angel Food Cake

¾ cup cake flour
4 heaping tablespoons Dutch process cocoa powder
1¼ cups sugar
1¼ cups egg whites (about 9 or 10 large eggs) at room temperature
¼ teaspoon salt
½ teaspoon cream of tartar
½ teaspoon vanilla extract
Coffee Sauce (recipe follows)

Put the baking rack in the center of the oven.

Preheat to 375 F.

Sift the flour and cocoa together until well-mixed. Add ¼ cup of the sugar and sift again into a large bowl; set aside.

In a clean bowl and using an electric mixer with clean beaters, gently whip the egg whites and salt. Add cream of tartar and increase mixer speed. Beat until soft peaks form when the beater is raised. Gradually beat in remaining 1 cup sugar until egg whites are stiff and glossy. Egg whites should not slide when the bowl is tipped.

Stir about 1 cup of egg whites into flour mixture. Pour in vanilla. Using a folding motion (and an old-fashioned angel food cake folder, if you have one) fold the egg whites into the flour.

Spoon half of remaining egg whites into mixture. Continue folding into flour and cocoa. It isn't necessary to incorporate every speck of flour, but avoid hard clumps of flour and cocoa.

Fold in remaining egg whites.

Make sure the flour and egg whites are well-incorporated. Pour the batter into an ungreased 10-inch tube pan with a removable center post. Smooth the top of the batter with a spatula.

Place pan in oven and bake for 35 minutes without opening the door. Test with a toothpick; it should come out clean and center should spring back when pressed lightly. (The center will rise above the pan during baking and sink like a souffle as the cake cools.)

Allow cake to cool evenly by suspending the pan from the neck of a soda or wine bottle (put the center hole of the cake pan through the neck of the bottle). Cool cake completely. It will take about 1½ hours.

Loosen the cake from the sides of the pan with a knife or metal spatula. Avoid moving the blade up and down as it rounds the cake. Simply press blade against cake sides. Invert cake on a serving plate.

To serve, slice the cake into wedges with a bread knife. Spoon a small amount of coffee sauce on each plate and top with a slice of cake. Garnish with powdered sugar, a coffee bean or mint leaf.

Makes 10 servings.

Nutrition information per serving without Coffee Sauce: calories, 188; fat, 0.2 gram; carbohydrate, 41.4 grams; cholesterol, 0 milligrams; sodium, 138 milligrams.

Coffee Sauce

½ cup confectioners' sugar

½ cup 1-percent milk

1 teaspoon cornstarch

2 tablespoons brandy, dark rum or Irish whiskey

2 tablespoons instant coffee powder

½ teaspoon vanilla extract

Beat together confectioners' sugar and milk. Bring to a boil. Remove from heat. Mix cornstarch, brandy and coffee powder into a thick paste. Stir into milk mixture. Return to heat, stirring constantly until mixture begins to thicken.

Immediately remove from heat. Stir in vanilla. Serve warm or at room temperature with Chocolate Angel Food Cake.

Makes 1½ cups.

Nutrition information per tablespoon: calories, 15; fat, 0.05 gram; carbohydrate, 2.8 grams; cholesterol, 0 milligrams; sodium, 2.3 milligrams.

■Warm bread pudding is a wonderful dessert on a chilly winter evening. This lemony version is not only delicious but virtually fat-free.

Bread Pudding With Brandy Sauce

Non-stick cooking spray
6 thick slices day-old oat bran, whole wheat or good quality French bread, torn into pieces
12 ounces evaporated skim milk
1 cup 1-percent milk
¼ cup egg substitutes
⅓ cup sugar
¼ teaspoon salt
⅛ teaspoon nutmeg
½ teaspoon grated fresh lemon peel
¼ cup golden raisins
¼ cup pitted dates, chopped
2 tablespoon sugar
Pinch of cream of tartar
3 egg whites

Preheat oven to 350 F.

Coat a baking dish with non-stick spray. Arrange the bread pieces in the dish. In a separate bowl, combine the evaporated skim milk, milk, egg substitutes, sugar, salt, nutmeg and lemon zest. Beat until the sugar has dissolved and the mixture is foamy.

Sprinkle with raisins and date pieces. Pour the milk and egg mixture over bread. Bake for 25 minutes.

While pudding is baking, beat the whites and cream of tartar until they begin to stiffen. Gradually sprinkle with remaining 2 tablespoons of sugar. Beat until whites become stiff and glossy. Remove pudding from oven and spoon meringue over top. Increase oven temperature to 400 F. Return pudding to oven and bake 6 to 8 minutes longer. Remove; allow to cool slightly while preparing Brandy Sauce.

Makes 6 servings.

Nutrition information per serving: calories, 254; fat, 2.3 grams; carbohydrate, 47.1 grams; cholesterol, 6 milligrams; sodium, 379 milligrams.

Brandy Sauce

½ cup confectioners' sugar
½ cup 1-percent milk
1 teaspoon cornstarch
2 teaspoons apple juice
2 tablespoons brandy, dark rum
   or orange liqueur
½ teaspoon vanilla extract

Beat together confectioners' sugar and milk. Bring to a boil. Remove from heat. Mix cornstarch and apple juice into a paste. Stir into milk mixture. Return to heat, stirring constantly until mixture begins to thicken.

Immediately remove from heat. Stir in brandy and vanilla. Serve warm over bread pudding.

Makes 6 servings.

Nutrition information per serving: calories, 61; fat, 0.2 gram; carbohydrate, 11.4 grams; cholesterol, 1 milligram; sodium, 10 milligrams.

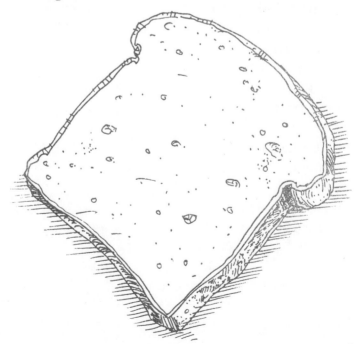

■ Lemon zest and lemon juice give this light cake a tangy flavor and a deep yellow hue. It stays moist and tasty even after it has been frozen.

Lemon Lover's Cake With Raspberry Sauce

Grated rind of 2 fresh lemons

3 tablespoons freshly squeezed lemon juice

2 cups sifted cake flour

½ teaspoon baking soda

2½ teaspoons baking powder

½ teaspoon salt

1½ cups sugar

½ cup corn oil

2 egg yolks

¾ cup buttermilk

¼ teaspoon lemon extract (optional)

8 egg whites (1 cup)

¼ teaspoon cream of tartar

Raspberry Sauce (recipe page 188)

Preheat oven to 325 F. Coat a 10-inch tube pan with a removable center post or 2 (8-inch) cake pans with non-stick cooking spray; set aside. Grate the lemons and combine with the lemon juice; set aside. Resift the cake flour with the baking soda, baking powder, salt and sugar. In a food processor or mixing bowl, combine the corn oil, yolks and buttermilk. Beat until smooth, then add the flour mixture by cups. Add the lemon mixture and lemon extract; set aside.

Using a mixer with clean and dry beaters, combine egg whites and cream of tartar. Beat at high speed until whites form stiff peaks. Turn bowl upside down; if whites do not slide, they are beaten enough.

Gently fold ⅓ of whites into batter; incorporate well. Fold in second ⅓ of whites and then remaining whites. Do not overbeat but there should be no streaks of white.

Pour the batter into prepared pan or pans. Rotate pan briskly to level the batter. Bake for 40 to 50 minutes or until a pick inserted in center comes out clean. Cool on a rack for 10 minutes. Run a knife around sides of mold to loosen. Invert cake on a rack and cool. Pour the Raspberry Sauce on serving plates and serve a slice of cake on top.

Makes 10 servings.

Test kitchen notes: The batter rises high during baking then falls back to form a dense, lemony cake with an almost pudding-like consistency.

Nutrition information per serving: calories, 326; fat, 12.2 grams; carbohydrate, 49.2 grams; cholesterol, 55 milligrams; sodium, 476 milligrams.

■ Fresh strawberries, a cinnamon-flavored crust and a creamy, vanilla-spiked filling combine to create a luxurious spring or summer dessert.

Strawberry Heart Tart

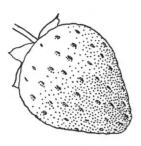

Crust:

1½ cups graham cracker crumbs (about 1 wax paper-wrapped pack of 10 graham crackers, crushed)

3 tablespoons soft margarine, melted

1 egg white

½ teaspoon vanilla

¼ teaspoon cinnamon

Filling:

1 (8-ounce) tub of reduced-calorie whipped cream cheese

2 tablespoons non-fat plain yogurt

¼ cup confectioners' sugar

¼ teaspoon freshly grated lemon rind

½ teaspoon vanilla

1 tablespoon orange liqueur or brandy

Topping:

2 pints fresh strawberries

¼ cup red currant jelly

Preheat oven to 325 F.

In a bowl, combine the graham cracker crumbs, margarine, egg white, vanilla and cinnamon. Stir to moisten all the crumbs. Press the mixture ⅛-inch thick on the bottom and sides of a 9-inch tart pan with a removable bottom. Bake for 12 to 15 minutes until crust is toasted and firm to the touch. Remove from oven and allow to cool.

To make filling, combine whipped cream cheese, yogurt, sugar, vanilla, lemon rind and orange liqueur or brandy in the bowl of a food processor or blender. Puree until smooth. Pour filling into crust and place in the freezer for 20 minutes or while preparing strawberries.

For the topping, wash the berries and allow them to dry on a paper towel. Remove the hulls. Arrange the berries, stem-side down, in a circle on the cream-cheese filling.

In a small microwave-safe dish or a saucepan, melt the red currant jelly to form a glaze. Allow to cool slightly. Using a pastry brush, coat each strawberry with jelly. Allow the excess to pool on the cream cheese.

Chill until ready to serve. This tart is best eaten within 2 hours after it's made.

Makes 6 servings.

Nutrition information per serving: calories, 308; fat, 14.4 grams; carbohydrate, 38.7 grams; cholesterol, 22 milligrams; sodium, 437 milligrams.

APPENDIX

Glossary

Al dente: An Italian term for pasta, that translates "to the tooth." It means the food should be soft but still have firmness and bite.

Balsamic: A type of slightly sweet, smooth-tasting Italian wine vinegar that has been aged in oak barrels. It is not sour like American vinegar and can be used alone on salads or vegetables or mixed into sauces and dressings. Balsamic vinegar is available in most grocery stores and specialty food markets.

Basil: A member of the mint family that adds a pungent, licorice flavor to food. It is used in Italian, French and American cooking. Use basil fresh or dry. Cook fresh leaves only briefly or use them raw as cooking destroys the flavor.

Beans: Any member of the pulse (peas) or legume family, which includes black-eyed peas, lentils, black beans, red beans and chick peas. High in soluble fiber, protein and minerals but low in fat and sodium.

Bean thread noodles: Also called cellophane noodles, these are made from the starch of the mung bean. Mung beans also produce the familiar bean sprouts. They should be soaked in hot water until they are pliable before using them in soups and braised dishes. Bean thread noodles have little taste but absorb the flavors of sauces they are served with. These noodles contain no eggs or fat.

Blue cornmeal: Cornmeal ground from a naturally blue native Southwestern corn, which retains it's color after cooking. Blue cornmeal is used in Southwestern-style cooking to make tortillas, muffins and breads.

Braise: A cooking method for meat or fibrous vegetables. Food is first browned in a small amount of oil, then simmered in a small amount of liquid (usually broth, wine or tomatoes) inside a tightly covered casserole. Foods can be braised in an oven or on the stovetop.

Breast: A whole chicken breast is composed of two halves. In this cookbook, the word stands for one-half of a chicken breast from the breastbone to the end of the ribs.

Canola oil: A highly polyunsaturated cooking oil made from rapeseed. One brand is Puritan.

Capers: The unopened flower buds of a caper shrub. The buds are pickled in brine and used to add a faintly sour zing to sauces, salads and dips. The best are the smallest or nonpareilles capers.

Chili oil: Cooking oil infused with hot red chili used as a seasoning in Chinese, Southeast Asian and Japanese cooking. A few drops are usually all that is necessary to add spice to dressings, sauces and dips.

Chayote: A hard, pear-shaped fruit with one oval seed that comes from the squash family. Frequently used in Latin American and Caribbean cooking. Also popular in Louisiana and Florida Cracker cooking. In Louisiana, chayotes are called mirletons or vegetable pears.

Chevre: A French term for all types of soft goat cheeses. Goat cheeses are much lower in fat and calories than most cow's milk cheeses. Soft goat cheeses are available in many well-stocked grocery stores and in specialty delicatessens.

Cilantro: The fresh leaves of the coriander plant which have a peppery, spicy flavor. Used frequently in Oriental, Latin American and Southwestern cooking.

Clam juice: A commercial shellfish-flavored broth used in soups and sauces. It is low in fat but high in sodium.

Conch: A large saltwater mollusk, similar to a snail, that lives in the warm waters of the Florida Keys and Caribbean. The large white foot is edible and the beautiful white-and-pink shell is used for horns and decorations. The conch is a protected species in Florida. Whelk or chopped clams may be substituted in most recipes.

Couscous: A tiny, Middle Eastern and North African pasta made from water and semolina flour and used like rice to make pilafs, side dishes and salads. Requires little cooking.

Cracker cooking: Simple Southern-style cooking as practiced by Florida's earliest settlers and designed to take advantage of ingredients at hand, such as wild cattle, greens and swamp cabbage (the heart of the sabal palm). Cracker cooking methods included barbecuing, stewing, baking and frying.

Cream of tartar: A byproduct of wine making, this acidic crystalline substance is used to stabilize beaten egg whites. It is also mixed with baking soda to make baking powder.

Cumin: A spice ground from the dried seeds of the cumin plant. This spice is used extensively in Latin American, Mexican, Indian and North African cooking.

Daikon: A large, mild white radish that is used in Japanese, Chinese and Southeast Asian cooking. It is thought to aid in digesting oily food. Though it's usually eaten raw, daikon can be cooked in soups and stews. Daikon is low in calories and fat and high in fiber.

Dijon-style mustard: A prepared mustard flavored with white wine that originated in Dijon, France. Domestic and imported brands are available in grocery stores.

Defatted: A term for removing the fat from a liquid by chilling it and scraping the congealed matter off the top.

Dredge or dust: To cover or coat food lightly with flour, cornmeal or cracker crumbs.

Evaporated skim milk: Canned skimmed milk that has been reduced by 60 percent in volume through evaporation. It has 9 milligrams of cholesterol and 1 gram of fat compared to evaporated whole milk, which has 74 milligrams of cholesterol and 19 grams of fat. Use to add a creamy thickness to soups, sauces and puddings.

Fish Sauce: A thin, salty, dark-brown flavoring agent used in Southeast Asian cooking instead of soy sauce. Called *nam pla* in Thailand and *nuoc nam* in Vietnam, it adds a subtle fish flavor to sauces. Thai brands are less salty.

Fold: A method of combining delicate ingredients such as egg whites or whipped cream, with thicker ingredients. Use a spatula or spoon in a circular motion, cutting through the mixture, scraping along the bottom of the bowl and bringing some of the mixture on the bottom to the top.

Garlic: A member of the lily family that includes onions, leeks, elephant garlic, green onions and shallots. All the members contain a natural chemical called allicin, which may inhibit blood clotting and aid in prevention of coronary heart disease. Garlic may be eaten raw or cooked.

Hoisin: A sweet-savory paste made from soybeans, garlic, five-spice powder and a small amount of chili. It's used in Chinese, Vietnamese and Thai cooking as a condiment like ketchup, or added to stir-fry dishes, barbecue sauces and dipping sauces.

Julienne: A method of cutting carrots, peppers, jicama, potatoes or other hard vegetables into matchstick slices. Place the vegetable on a board, slice in half lengthwise and into long, thin strips.

Key limes: Small, very tart limes with a yellowish skin that are grown in the Florida Keys, Caribbean and West Indies. They are used to make Key Lime Pie marinades and sauces.

Marsala: An amber-colored, fortified wine made in western Sicily. Dry Marsala is used to make sauces for chicken and veal dishes. The sweet variety is the main flavoring of Italian *zabaglione,* a dessert sauce.

Mirin: Mirin is a sweet, syrupy Japanese rice wine used to sweeten salad dressings, sauces and simmered foods. It is used in teriyaki or grilled dishes to add a brown glaze. Mirin is available in most groceries and Oriental markets.

Oat bran: The outer husk of the oat grain that is high in water-soluble fiber. Because of the water-soluble fiber, it is thought to lower blood cholesterol levels when at least 2 ounces are eaten daily.

Pectin: A water-soluble carbohydrate found in the skin and white rind of fruits, such as apples, cranberries and citrus. It is also a natural gel that thickens jams and jellies.

Puree: To chop food so finely in a blender, food processor or food mill that it becomes a smooth, thick sauce. A puree is also a sauce made from pureed vegetables, fruit, seafood or meat.

Reduce: To decrease the volume of a liquid by rapid boiling in an uncovered pan. As the volume decreases, the flavors intensify and the consistency thickens. Reduction sauces can be very flavorful yet lower in fat than sauces made with cream, flour or eggs.

Rice vermicelli: Also called rice sticks, these are thin Oriental noodles made from rice flour and water. They're available in a variety of sizes and thicknesses. They should be soaked in hot water until they're soft and pliable before being used in hot or cold dishes. They contain no fat.

Rice vinegar: A mild, white, pleasant-tasting Oriental vinegar made from rice and alcohol. Far less sour than American vinegars, it can be used without oil on salads or cooked vegetables and added to sauces and soups. It is available in Oriental markets and the ethnic foods section of most grocery stores.

Ricotta: A cheese product made from the whey drained from provolone and mozzarella. It is bland and has a soft consistency. Brands made from part-skim milk are low in fat and cholesterol. Use in pasta dishes, dips and desserts.

Roux: A blend of oil or butter and flour used to thicken sauces and gravies. The oil or butter are mixed together over heat and a liquid is whisked in. As the liquid reaches the boiling point it binds with the flour and thickens into a sauce.

Scotch bonnet pepper: A fiery, tiny, round chili pepper that is used in Jamaican cooking.

Tahini: A smooth, nutty tasting paste made from ground sesame seeds. Similar to peanut butter, small amounts can be used in sauces, Middle Eastern recipes and Oriental noodle dishes.

Wheat germ: The highly nutritious embryo of the wheat kernel which is milled away in the production of white flour. It is sold in grocery stores and health food markets.

Zest: The colored exterior peel of citrus fruits that contains highly flavored oils. Zest is used to add citrus flavor to sauces, cakes, baking and frozen desserts. Orange and lemon zest are the most commonly used in recipes. Avoid using the zest of Key limes, which becomes bitter.

MENU PLANNING

Festive holiday dinner

Turban of Sole With Salmon Mousse (page 65)
Turkey Montmorency (page 107)
Mashed Sweet Potatoes (page 91)
Chevre-Stuffed Tomatoes (page 135)
Bread Pudding With Brandy Sauce (page 196)

Bridal shower luncheon

Tortellini With Pesto Dipping Sauce (page 13)
Fresh Tuna Salad Nicoise (page 43)
Whole-Wheat Breadsticks (page 168)
Watermelon Chiffon Pie (page 177)

After symphony dinner

French Onion Soup (page 20)
Crab and Artichoke Lasagna (page 63)
Mint Coleslaw With Mint Vinaigrette (page 32)
Chocolate Angel Food Cake With Coffee Sauce (page 194)

Before an Orlando Magic game

Vegetable Tray served with Greek Hummus Dip (7), Red-Hot Dip (page 5) and Tapenade Spread (page 3)
Turkey Burgers With Cranberry Ketchup (page 117) and Oven Fries (page 156)
Honey Peanut Butter Granola Bars (page 180)

Weekday family dinner

Geechee Oysters and Rice (page 58)
Corn Bread (page 166)
Glazed Carrots and Parsnips (page 140)
Oatmeal Cookies (page 182)

Microwave dinner

Chilled Gazpacho (page 18) With Whole-Wheat Breadsticks (page 168)
Sole With Mushrooms, Artichokes and Almonds (page 50)
Mardi Gras Slaw (page 33) With Creamy Pineapple Dressing(page 151)

Orange Cheesecake With Raspberry Sauce (page 187)

Fourth of July picnic

Black and White Bean Salad (page 28)
Sweet Potato Salad With Honey Vinaigrette Dressing (page 24)
Pork Tenderloin With Cilantro Mayonnaise (page 95)
Rock Shrimp Rockefeller (page 59)
Fish Marinated in Vinegar and Vegetables (page 61)
Sunflower Oat Bran Muffins (page 163)
Oat Bran Carrot Cake With Cream Cheese Frosting (page 189)

Summer dinner party

Artichokes With Raspberry Vinaigrette (page 138)
Grilled Corn Chowder With Clams (page 19)
Ginger Glazed Salmon With Sushi Rice Pancakes (page 45)
Seasonal green vegetables
Peach Ice Cream (page 184) With Raspberry Sauce (page 188)

Tailgate picnic

Vegetable Batter Bread (page 171)
Eggplant With Green Chili and Cheese (page 137)
Chicken Picadillo Enchiladas (page 109)
Tossed Vegetables With Pecan Dressing (page 34)
Chocolate Citrus Cake (page 183)

Poolside or Lakeside Fiesta

Lobster and Crab Ceviche (page 56)
Picadillo al Horno (page 83)
New Mexican Blue Corn Muffins (page 164)
Mantequilla de Pobre (page 143)
Postre de Mousse (page 173)

A

B

C